RSPB Guide to
WATCHING
·BRITISH·
BIRDS

RSPB Guide to
WATCHING
·BRITISH·
BIRDS

Peter Conder • David Saunders

Hamlyn
London·NewYork·Sydney·Toronto

Acknowledgements

Illustrated by Peter Hayman and Norman Arlott
Identification plates by Noel Cusa

Colour Photographs

Aerofilms Ltd: 78 top; *Ardea*: 27 bottom, 71 bottom, J. A. Bailey
74-75 bottom, I. Beames 27 top, J. B. & S. Bottomley 22 top, M. D. England
67 bottom; *Frank V. Blackburn*: 26, 38 bottom, 66 bottom, 70;
Bruce Coleman Ltd: S. Dalton 79, Dennis Green 31 bottom, D. & K. Urry
30 top, 31 top, J. van Wormer 74-75 top; *Eric Hosking*: 19 top and bottom,
27 bottom, 66 top, 67 top, 78 bottom; *Jacana*: 23; *Natural History
Photographic Agency*: J. Jeffrey 71 top; *Wildlife Studies Ltd*: 18 top.

Black and White Photographs

Ardea: 50, Ian Beames 28, J. B. & S. Bottomley 49, C. R. Knights 62,
J. P. Laub 61; *Peter Conder*: 36; *Eric Hosking*: 48, 60; *Natural History
Photographic Agency*: D. N. Dalton 72; *Royal Society for the Protection
of Birds*: Richard T. Mills 73.

Published by The Hamlyn Publishing Group Limited
London · New York · Sydney · Toronto
Astronaut House, Feltham, Middlesex, England

ISBN 0 600 30583 X
Printed in Italy

The material in this book previously appeared in
RSPB Guide to Birdwatching and *RSPB Guide to British
Birds*, published by The Hamlyn Publishing Group Limited.

Contents

Introduction

The ability to fly allows birds to escape from predators relatively easily, whilst their keen senses of sight and hearing also help them to become aware of possible danger quickly. Consequently they have less need to remain inconspicuous than do many other wild animals such as mammals. Furthermore, many species have evolved bright plumage for territorial and mating purposes. These factors, together with the general abundance of many species, mean that birds are probably the most popular group of animals among nature watchers.

This book is designed to enable both the beginner and the more experienced birdwatcher to identify many of Britain's most commonly encountered species. But putting a name to each bird often involves understanding something of their lives, and this book also provides a thorough introduction to the many aspects of bird structure, behaviour and ecology upon which sound observation and identification is often based. Thus there are chapters on territory, song and courtship as well as chapters which discuss, for example, the choice of birdwatching equipment, and how to ensure birds visit your garden.

One does not have to go far in order to see a variety of species – indeed, no further than our windows, for quite a number visit our gardens and many not normally encountered there may be attracted by the provision of food and water. This is just as possible to achieve in cities and towns as it is in the open countryside. City parks are ideal for both birds and their watchers, while there can be few people who do not live within reach of a gravel pit or reservoir. Those able to travel will soon discover that fine estuaries, islands and moorland are all easily accessible, opening up for the birdwatcher a new range of habitats and the different birds which they support.

In this book over 200 British birds are described and illustrated, the birds in the identification section being divided into five groups – ducks, geese and swans; water birds; seabirds; birds of prey; and land birds – which are indicated by an at-a-glance reference system of coloured borders.

This book combines the talents of two highly respected and experienced ornithologists and authors. Peter Conder is a former director of the RSPB with a lifetime's involvement in birdwatching. David Saunders was for seven years warden of Skomer National Natural Reserve, and was also organizer of the huge seabird census of 'Operation Seafarer', which mapped and counted every seabird colony in the British Isles.

Equipment

Field notebooks

Together with a pair of binoculars and a field guide the most important aid that a birdwatcher will need is a field notebook, which is used to record the essential facts of any observation, as well as comments or impressions while they are still fresh in the mind.

The field notebook may take a number of different forms, although it obviously must be small enough to fit easily into your pocket. It may be a cheap notebook that you can throw away when it is filled and the information has been transferred to a more permanent system of recording. On the other hand a pocket-sized loose-leaf notebook can be very useful as the sheets can be transferred directly into one of the structural index systems.

It is in the field notebook that you write the details of your sightings. You should never be afraid of recording too much at this stage, as you can analyze and edit the entry when you are writing up your final records. Remember that every observation in the field is unrepeatable. Always record the date, time and place together with the weather conditions. An Ordnance Survey grid map-reference is a useful method of recording the place of your observation. It is also worth noting the number of the ten kilometre square in which you are working since it is often useful for recording the distribution of birds. Another way of recording your observations is by using a portable tape-recorder; this has the advantage of leaving your hands and eyes free to manipulate your binoculars and watch the bird. However, some practice is needed as initially one tends to overuse it.

Final records

Whether you write up your records or simply transfer them to another notebook or filing system depends on how you prefer to organize your original observations and, of course, whether the original field notes are legible. Some people never write up the results of their observations, and, indeed, there is little that would need to be done to a simple list of birds. Some birdwatchers, however, like to go further and keep a diary of ornithological events. In one way the 'bird diary' is the simplest method of keeping more permanent records, but it is not always the easiest system from which to retrieve information. In addition to a Lefax field notebook I, personally, use a stiff-backed notebook and write out an index at the end of each volume.

With a loose-leaf system, as with the loose-leaf field notebook, the sheets

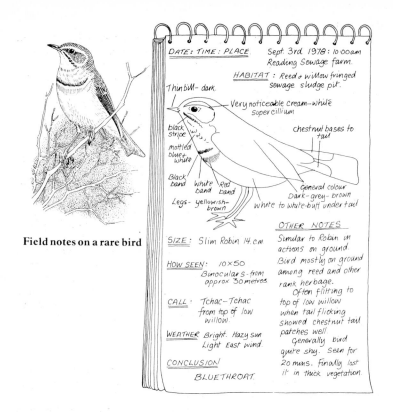

Field notes on a rare bird

DATE: TIME: PLACE — Sept. 3rd 1978: 10:00am Reading Sewage farm.

HABITAT: Reed & willow fringed sewage sludge pit.

Thin bill - dark.

Very noticeable cream--white Super cillium

black stripe

chestnut bases to tail

mottled blue+ white

Black band White band Red band

General colour Dark-grey-brown

Legs- yellowish-brown

white to white-buff under tail

SIZE: Slim Robin 14.cm

HOW SEEN: 10×50 Binoculars - from approx 30 metres.

CALL: Tchac-Tchac from top of low willow.

WEATHER: Bright. Hazy sun Light East wind.

CONCLUSION

BLUETHROAT.

OTHER NOTES

Similar to Robin in actions on ground. Bird mostly on ground among reed and other rank herbage. Often flitting to top of low willow when tail flicking showed chestnut tail patches well. Generally bird quite shy. Seen for 20 mins. Finally lost it in thick vegetation.

Whenever you see a bird you cannot identify you should write a full description of its plumage, shape, behaviour, calls and habitat before you refer to a field guide.

can be re-arranged according to your needs; for example, all the records on a particular species or a specific locality can be kept together. What you record depends on what interests you. If you are a beginner identification problems will almost certainly require you to write down bird descriptions and the excitement of discovering new birds will be reflected in your diary. Later sections and chapters in this book should give you other ideas. But one thing is clear: writing down what one has seen is a wonderful way of developing observational ability and an enquiring mind. All too often I realize what I have not recorded when I come to write-up the field notes, and all too often when I look back for information from old records I find that I have failed to make a note about some important item. So regular recordings, and regular checking of what one has written, helps to improve one's field discipline.

Bird listing

Once you can be sure of identifying most of the common birds that you see in your normal 'birding' area, or, indeed, even as you are learning, you will want a list of birds that you have seen, so that you can read more about them when you get home. Lists can also remind you later of what you have seen in a particular place and are useful when you visit it again.

However, field lists have an additional value if you use them properly. Many regional clubs produce annual reports based on the records submitted by their members, and here the figures recorded in the field list can be the basis of the records sent to the county recorder.

It is possible to purchase from the British Trust for Ornithology printed field lists which have a space for the date, the length of time you spend in any particular habitat, description of the weather, the habitat and a column for numbers or a symbol opposite each bird's name. The symbol may just be a tick to show that you have seen the bird or it may be a figure indicating the number of birds you have counted. The British Trust for Ornithology have three different types of field lists. The first contains the names of a hundred common birds. The second list is the *Field List of British Birds*, and contains the names of all those species recorded in Great Britain and Ireland at least three times a year, in recent years. The third includes all the species that have occurred in Western Europe, North Africa and the Near East. It is a particularly useful list especially when travelling abroad in search of birds. Perhaps the most common use of the field list is for keeping records of birds seen on an outing.

Binoculars

No real birdwatcher will be without a pair of binoculars. These are usually essential for the proper identification of a bird and will help considerably in the observation of close detail such as feeding methods and habits.

There are enormous numbers of binoculars on the market and choosing a pair which is going to suit your needs and pocket needs careful thought. The most useful guide to choosing binoculars is the BTO's *Binoculars, Telescopes and Cameras*, Guide No. 14, by J. J. M. Flegg and D. E. Glue and, even if you are being advised by another expert, it is certainly well worth reading.

The points that guide you in your choice are the magnification, the field of view, the optical quality of the lenses, weight, size and finally, no doubt, cost; you should have all these points in mind when choosing. For general birdwatching, which means that one day you may be watching in a wood and the next by an estuary, binoculars which magnify $8 \times$, $9 \times$ and $10 \times$ are the best. Below this the magnification of the image is so small as to be nearly worthless, and with higher magnification you will not only be magnifying the image of the bird but also the shakiness of your hands and the effort of the wind buffeting your binoculars. Some people can manage to hold $12 \times$ binoculars but once you get above this magnification you really need to be able to fix your binoculars to a tripod or some firm base.

The second point to be considered is the field of view which is linked to the amount of light gathered by the objective lens of the binoculars. The wider the objective lens the better the light-gathering power and the better you will be able to see in poor light. Generally, the most commonly used binoculars for birdwatching have objective lenses with a diameter of somewhere between 30–50 millimetres. The number of times that a pair of binoculars magnifies and the diameter of the objective lens produce the figures which are found on glasses (e.g. 8×30, 9×40, 10×50) and from these figures it is possible to gain some idea of the suitability of the glasses for use in poor light. If you divide the magnification into the figure for the width of the objective lens, the higher the answer you obtain the more suitable the binoculars are for use in poor light. In fact, the result should be higher than four for hand-held binoculars. Lenses which have been coated with a non-reflecting material, or which are said to be 'bloomed', usually have superior light-transmitting properties so a figure as low as four is passable with these lenses.

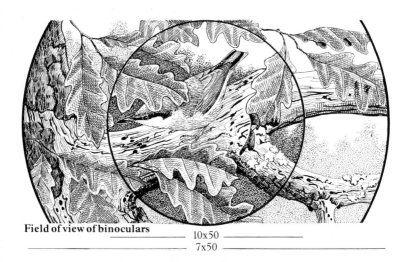

Field of view of binoculars
——————————— 10x50 ———————————
————————————————— 7x50 —————————————————

When choosing binoculars a compromise may be necessary between high magnification and field of view. This drawing shows how the field of view decreases with magnification.

Generally speaking, the field of view decreases with increasing magnification but increases with the diameter of the objective lens. A wide field of vision is particularly helpful when you are trying to watch and follow a bird in dense cover, for instance in a woodland. The field of view for 8×30 binoculars is normally 120m at 1000m (390ft at 3280ft).

The optical quality of a pair of binoculars is very difficult to assess when buying for the first time. This is really where the help of an experienced person is necessary. You need the best resolution of detail over all the field of view. With cheaper glasses the resolution may fall away at the edges, and on some glasses you can see colour fringes where the image is surrounded by a faint colour halo; these should be avoided.

Finally, do not get binoculars which are too big to hold in your hands or which feel heavy when you are handling them in the shop, because they will feel even heavier on your neck after an hour or so of birdwatching, and your hands and arms will soon tire trying to hold them steady in front of your eyes.

The more money you can afford to pay the better the chances are that you will get a pair of binoculars which have a good lens system and reliable mechanics which should last you a lifetime. However, today it is possible to buy reliable and relatively inexpensive binoculars.

Some binoculars are equipped with zoom lenses which enable you to find a bird at low magnification and, when you have located it, boost the magnification to obtain a better view. These are, I think, of dubious merit as there is another mechanical piece to go wrong; they add weight and, possibly, also delay in obtaining a good view of a bird which may only be perched momentarily.

Telescopes

While binoculars are almost essential to birdwatching, telescopes become useful, if not essential, when you become really interested and need a high magnification to identify or watch birds at long distances, for example, on estuaries and at sea.

Prismatic telescopes are more expensive than the tube telescopes but I think that their better resolution of detail makes them well worth the extra cost. They are of a fixed length and focus is usually achieved by a small milled knob. Some prismatic telescopes also have 'zoom' eye-pieces which means that, once you have found the target bird, you can twist that part of the eye-piece and increase the magnification.

The magnification provided by a telescope usually ranges from about $20 \times$ to $60 \times$. However, as the magnification increases the amount of light being transmitted through the lens is reduced, unless the diameter of the object glass is also increased enormously.

Greater magnification, as in binoculars, increases the problems caused by hand-shake and a firm but light tripod with a pan and tilt head is absolutely essential to hold the telescope steady. Incidentally, it should ideally be a black one so that light is not reflected back to the bird you are trying to watch.

Clothing

The first point to remember is that although you wish the bird no harm you are in fact a 'hunter' – a hunter of facts about live birds. You do not wish to kill but to observe as closely as possible without frightening the bird. Bright colours for birdwatching, such as the orange or yellow cagoules, therefore, are out. You need to be clothed in greens, browns and greys or the natural colour of that part of the countryside in which you are working. Khaki is an ideal colour; dark greens, olive and browns are also good as a general rule but can stick out conspicuously on a beach or sand dune. Camouflage jackets, suits and hats, which are regularly advertised in the sporting magazines, are extremely useful. The correct sort of outer garments are more often obtainable at a gunsmith's than at a normal clothing store. A hat is essential, particularly if you are fair-haired, but it is also important to break up the outline of your head, to hide your eyes and shade and darken your face. Pigeon-shooters sometimes use a camouflaged face-mask in order to hide the brightly coloured splodge of their face and, if they do it, why should not a keen birdwatcher?

Whilst soberly coloured clothing is important, there should also be a strong tone contrast between garments – a darker coat with lighter-coloured trousers or vice versa. A patterned material is less conspicuous than a plain one, and a symmetrical object tends to be more conspicuous than an asymmetrical one; also, it is particularly important to disguise the shape of your head and shoulders. An easy way to see what I mean is to observe others when they are birdwatching. Which outfits merge best against a wood or a field, and which part of the body sticks out like a sore thumb? Then decide what could be done to make the other person blend in with the countryside. Nine times out of ten it is the pale face of the observer which is most obvious on an otherwise camouflaged person. The best camouflage is made more effective by absolute stillness and slow and gentle movements.

On many of its reserves the RSPB has built hides. However, the reason for wearing naturally coloured clothes and disguising one's features is to obviate the need for a hide when you are birdwatching. Hides are essential for close-up photography or making a detailed study of the nesting behaviour of some species. They are also useful if you are studying an open area such as a pond, but the average birdwatcher will not normally wish to carry a hide around with him. On the other hand, camouflage nets are fairly easy to carry in a haversack. A number of ex-Government nets are still advertised in shooting magazines but they are also easily made using a length of netting (approximately 3×15m [10×50ft] with a 5cm [2in] mesh). At regular intervals strips of grey, brown and green material can be tied to the net. There should be sufficient strips to disguise the observer's outline from the bird while allowing a clear view through the net. Again stillness adds to the effectiveness of the natural coloration. The net can be simply draped over the head and shoulders or tied between trees or bushes.

A second point about clothing is comfort. In winter the pleasure of watching birds can be ruined by getting wet and very chilled. With the waterproof garments available these days it is possible to remain dry even in the heaviest rain, and many coats of suitable colours lined with quilt for extra warmth are advertised in bird and country magazines. Thermal underclothes can also be highly effective during the cold winter months. Some people like cagoules, but for myself I find that they are too noisy, particularly in cold weather, the rustling does not always frighten birds but it does make it much more difficult to hear them. A birdwatcher would never choose for birdwatching some of the fluorescent colours in which cagoules are made for climbers. However, if you are climbing or indulging in some occupation involving risk, you must observe the safety rules for that occupation.

Feet must be kept warm and dry. Whilst it is easy to keep feet dry by using rubber boots it can sometimes be a problem to keep them warm especially if a lot of standing about is entailed. It is now possible to buy socks made of polyester-filled quilted nylon which are especially designed for use in rubber boots and which are extremely effective.

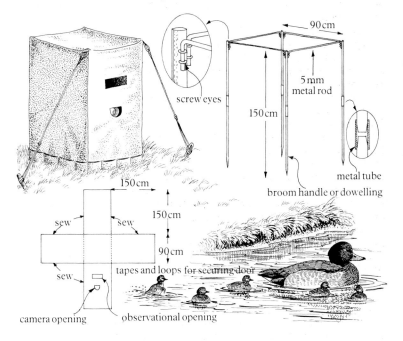

When using a hide near a nest great care must be taken to move it closer in slow stages so that the birds become accustomed to it.

Photography

Photography is an enormous subject about which many books have already been written. Two are *Wildlife Photography* written by Eric Hosking and John Gooders, and *An Introduction to Bird and Wildlife Photography* by John Marchington and Anthony Clay.

Many birdwatchers use the 35 millimetre single-lens reflex camera. Usually when taking photographs of habitats a 50 millimetre lens is needed but a wide-angled 35 millimetre lens will also give extremely good results. For photographing birds at a distance a long-focus or telephoto lens is essential; lenses with a focal point of 300 or 400 millimetres are most commonly used.

With these lenses a fast shutter speed is necessary, at the very least 1/250 of a second, together with a fast film. However, as you increase the speed you also increase the 'grain' of the processed film emulsion thus losing some of the definition. A useful piece of equipment is a shoulder butt on which to mount the camera, this helps to keep the camera from shaking while still allowing you a great deal of flexibility. If you are in a position to use your camera with a tripod then a slower shutter setting is possible. Having acquired the basic camera you can build up the remainder of your equipment as and when the money becomes available and the need arises.

If you intend to photograph birds at their nest or in more open positions a hide is almost essential. It is possible to buy one but a simple construction is easily within the reach of the average handyman. The photographer must be extremely careful in his approach to the nest and the way he uses his hide. It is important to remember that the welfare of the bird must be your first concern. *The Nature Photographer's Code of Practice* published by the RSPB and the Zoological Photographic Society can be obtained from the RSPB on receipt of a large stamped addressed envelope. Remember, too, that the Wildlife and the Countryside Act 1981 prohibits the disturbance of birds on the First Schedule to the Act. The RSPB publishes a booklet giving the information as to which birds are covered by this law and where you should write for a licence.

Tape-recording

For me, the tape-recorder is a way of recording an event and I use it both for dictating notes in the field and recording bird sound. With a portable cassette recorder and the correct type of microphone it is possible to make adequate recordings in the field for very little expense. Although convenient for handling in the field these smaller tape-recorders do not produce a very high quality recording. Results can be improved, however, by using a parabolic reflector which collects and concentrates more sound than the microphone alone. It also adds some direction to the microphone and helps to cut out unwanted background noise. For those who wish to go further with this pursuit Richard Margoschis' *Recording Natural History Sounds* (1977) covers most aspects of recording.

Sound guides

One of the great delights of birdwatching are the sweet and varied songs and calls that some birds can produce whether it is simply the song of a Robin or the raucous chorus of seabirds on their cliffs or the murmur of thousands of ducks as they loaf and feed on some undisturbed lake. Since every species has its individual vocabulary, your ability to identify a bird's song and its calls can add greatly to your efficiency as a birdwatcher.

There are a number of recordings on the market either on record or cassette tape. A set of these recordings is most useful in early spring for reminding you of the songs and calls of the summer visitors, particularly the ones which are so difficult to differentiate, like the Garden Warbler and the Blackcap or the Sedge and Reed Warblers. Some of the best recordings are to be found in the following records or cassettes.

The BBC have produced a whole range of discs and cassettes, some mono and others stereo, of a wide range of wildlife recordings including a twelve-inch disc *British Wild Birds in Stereo*. Also available is *Woodland and Garden Birds* which can be bought on two cassettes or mono discs.

Bird Concerts, produced by the Roché Institute, consists of recordings of birds of different habitats from various parts of the world. They make a very useful series for the traveller-birdwatcher. The *Shell Nature Series* consists of nine records of over one hundred species of birds and is arranged according to habitat. Finally there are two less pretentious recordings which are worth considering Richard Margoschis has produced a stereo cassette entitled *British Wildlife Habitats No 1* with natural sounds from eight different habitats; and *Wildlife Sound Tracks* on eight cassettes is recorded and privately published by John Kirby, Drummond Cottage, Aysgarth, Leyburn, North Yorkshire DL8 3AH.

How to meet people
Unless you are a complete 'loner' you can increase your enjoyment of birdwatching by joining one of the bird societies, clubs, or RSPB members' groups which exist in most counties and larger towns. The main function of such clubs is to stimulate an interest in the birds of that county by means of lectures, field excursions, surveys and regular bulletins of recently recorded birds. Joining such a club is well worthwhile as it allows you to meet others who are interested in birdwatching and also gives you the opportunity to contribute to the work of the club.

The Royal Society for the Protection of Birds is the largest society of its kind in the country, if not in the world, with over a quarter of a million members. Its chief function is to ensure the better protection of wild birds and to create a public awareness in birds and their place in nature. Its reserves protect almost 40,000 hectares of bird habitat which can be visited daily and also require voluntary help from people who are prepared to spend a week or so wardening and helping with the general management of the reserves. Whether you are a 'bird-lover' or an expert ornithologist you ought to belong to the RSPB. The address of its head office is The Lodge, Sandy, Bedfordshire SG19 2DL.

Once you have passed through the early stages of identifying birds and have become interested in asking and answering questions about birds and joining others to help answer those questions you should join the British Trust for Ornithology. This national organization apart from stimulating and organizing a lot of very useful field research has three conferences a year which can be well worth attending.

How to identify birds

When you start learning to identify birds it is best to use this book, which features a limited number of species. This reduces the chance of you confusing, say, a common garden bird with a rare visitor from abroad. In the illustration opposite you will find the usual names of the different feathers, including those of the upper and undersides of the bird's wing. Names such as scapulars and axillaries appear rather daunting at first but most of them are used fairly regularly amongst birdwatchers.

Many warblers, waders and other species have eye and supercilary stripes of various lengths, colours and thicknesses. It has been suggested that they help the bird to aim its beak at a particle of food. The edge of the black cap of many species may have the same effect. Another part of the bird to which particular attention should be paid are the wings and the coverts which are smallish feathers of different shapes and sizes lying over the bases of the primary and secondary flight feathers. You need to know them because they or their tips may be coloured differently from the remainder of the wing and thus produce the wing bars which can be prominent field marks.

Field marks
Field marks are one of the major aids to identification and are any conspicuous features in a bird's plumage or shape. They can be prominent patches of colour such as the red of a cock Bullfinch's breast, its blue-black cap or its white rump. Other field marks may be the presence of wing bars, white outer tail-feathers or a forked tail or curved bill or indeed anything which is conspicuous. Some may be hidden when the bird is at rest. The Redwing's red flanks can be seen only partially and the Grey Plover's black patch on its axillaries cannot be seen until the bird actually lifts its wings and flies. Another point to watch for is that some colours are not what they seem: for instance, is the colour that you see on the Starling in sunlight the true colour of its feathers or is it due to iridescence? Iridescence is caused by the physical nature of the structure of the barbules which interferes with the normal refraction of light from the feather surface. Adult Starlings, Magpies, Lapwings, and the drakes of several species of wildfowl have this type of plumage. Also remember that the evening sun often casts a red tinge and you can, if you forget this, see some most extraordinarily coloured birds. Describing colours is always rather difficult and I try to remember the colour makers' names for artists' colours which are fairly uniform.

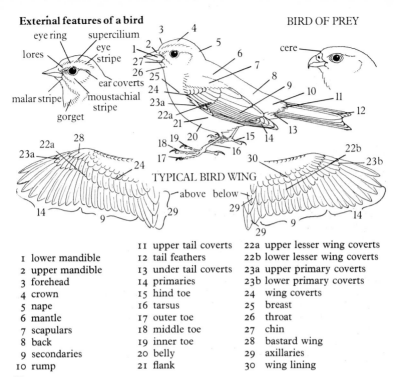

External features of a bird

BIRD OF PREY

eye ring superscilium

lores eye stripe

malar stripe ear coverts moustachial stripe

gorget

TYPICAL BIRD WING

above below

cere

1 lower mandible	11 upper tail coverts	22a upper lesser wing coverts
2 upper mandible	12 tail feathers	22b lower lesser wing coverts
3 forehead	13 under tail coverts	23a upper primary coverts
4 crown	14 primaries	23b lower primary coverts
5 nape	15 hind toe	24 wing coverts
6 mantle	16 tarsus	25 breast
7 scapulars	17 outer toe	26 throat
8 back	18 middle toe	27 chin
9 secondaries	19 inner toe	28 bastard wing
10 rump	20 belly	29 axillaries
	21 flank	30 wing lining

Size

A note on size is important in your field description. Field guides usually give the length in centimetres or inches at the beginning of every section. This is generally the measurement of a specimen placed flat on its back and taken from the tip of its beak to the end of its tail. As you do not usually see a bird in the field like this, it is better to try and compare the size with another species known to you. The size of flying birds is notoriously difficult to judge even for experienced birdwatchers.

Shape

Shape is a give-away feature in many species. Is, for instance, the body of the bird you have seen, tubby and upright like a Robin or slim and horizontal like a Wagtail? Is it long-legged? Does it have a long neck or a long tail? As you become more experienced you will get to know many birds by their shape. You will obviously be able to tell that a certain bird is a duck but you will also be able to tell a Wigeon by its pronounced forehead or a Pintail by its long thin neck and needle-like tail. You will also be able to distinguish the Mallard by its cocked-up tail from the Pochard with its more rounded body and tail that lies almost on the water. Another way of learning bird shapes is to draw

17

ELEONORA'S FALCON *Falco eleonorae* L 14" W 36"

HOBBY *Falco subbuteo* L 11/12" W 27-30"

MERLIN *Falco columbarius* L 11/12" W 24-26"

18

Left The Bullfinch is a widespread British resident which prefers areas with plenty of thick cover. Note the heavy, seed-eating bill.

Left One of the field guides that has made field identification comparatively easy to masses of birdwatchers throughout Europe. The *Country Life Guide* has the advantage of text facing the plates.

Right above and right Camouflage is in effect a portable hide. The camouflaged human observer is making himself less recognizable to birds, particularly if he keeps still. Brightly coloured clothes are valuable where a recreation is hazardous — but for most birdwatching drab colours are best.

them. Drawing birds makes you concentrate on essential details and teaches you to look at them in a different and refreshing way.

Movement

The way a bird moves must be noted and, when considered with the shape, can be a diagnostic feature. Was it walking, one foot down after the other, comparatively slowly, or running with 'twinkling' feet? When searching for food, larger birds usually walk. Large waders like Oystercatchers, Curlews and godwits, as well as Ravens, Rooks, ducks and geese, all tend to walk. Plovers can run for short distances then they stop, look and listen. Smaller waders like the Sanderling 'twinkle' or run with 'twinkling' feet along the edge of the waves while Dunlins twist and turn digging busily and deeply into the wet sand or soft mud. On a lawn the Pied Wagtail may rush about after flying insects; in contrast, Chaffinches are sedate walkers. Blackbirds and Song Thrushes, like most of their family, hop or run and hop – the Blackbird when displaying to an intruder and therefore somewhat excited, runs, adopting a rather special posture of the body known as the 'rodent run'.

When you see a flock of small birds feeding amongst the branches, what is their method of locomotion? Do they sidle up the twigs like some of the warblers or hop from branch to branch or twig to twig like the tits? On tree trunks, two or three species may hunt together – how do they climb the tree? Do they circle gradually up the trunk or do they go straight up? Once they have got to the top of one tree how do they get to the bottom of another? The Treecreeper, for instance, rarely climbs down a tree: once it has climbed fairly high it will fly to the bottom of another tree and even to the bottom of the tree it has just climbed, while the Nuthatch can walk down.

Some birds fly in a very distinctive manner. Once you have learnt the regular and deep rounded wing beats of the Lapwing, flashing black and white, you will be able to identify it so long as you can see movement of the wings. The commonest feature to notice is whether the flight is level or undulating: finches, buntings and wagtails all have an undulating flight caused by the bird beating its wings for a second or two and then closing them. Each species has its own flight pattern depending upon the speed and number of wing beats. The Grey Heron flies swiftly and directly across the sky, and its slow wing beats deceive you as to its speed over the ground. Geese fly in lines or in V-shape formations, Woodpigeons in loose flocks, Buzzards soar and wheel, Kestrels hover, while Swallows and martins wheel, swirl and chatter over water-meadows and villages.

When you look at water birds, how do they swim? Do they sit high in the water like Geese or low like Shags? How do they dive? Do they slip under the water or jacknife themselves out of the water to gain impetus?

Range and habitat

Two other factors that need to be taken into account when identifying birds are geographical range and the habitat in which the bird has been found.

If you identify a species which is not normally present in the area in which

Bird shapes

Grey Heron

Mallard

Kestrel

Lapwing

Woodpigeon

Herring Gull

Tawny Owl

Great Spotted Woodpecker

Whitethroat

Swallow

Swift

Chaffinch

Robin

With experience you will be able to identify families, genera and even some species merely by their shape alone.

Above No other bird hovers in quite the same way as the Kestrel. Notice that its head seems fixed to one spot whilst the body will move about in relation to wind strength and direction.

Below The Curlew's long down-curved bill separates it from all but the rather rarer Whimbrel, but its call – 'coorwee' – identifies it at once. Nests on moorlands but winters on estuaries and often on rocky coasts.

The red-billed Chough searching for ants with its down-curved bill amongst clifftop Thrift on the western cliffs of the British Isles, is one of the ornithological thrills — a unique bird on a rugged coastline.

you are birdwatching it would be wise to re-check your identification and make sure you have an adequate field description and then report your sighting to your county recorder.

A bird's habitat is not really a diagnostic feature as, particularly on migration, birds can turn up in all sorts of places, but it can be an indication. For example, if you find a yellowish-bellied wagtail on a water meadow in south-east England it is more likely to be a Yellow Wagtail than a Grey Wagtail. In Wales you are more likely to see a Grey Wagtail along rocky streamsides. With large groups of birds such as ducks each species will differ in its choice of habitat. Amongst the ducks, for instance, some prefer saltwater such as the Scoters and Long-tailed Ducks whereas Pochards and Tufted Ducks prefer freshwater. Amongst the waders, Purple Sandpipers and Turnstones forage mostly on the seashore whereas a lot of waders may be just as much at home on a freshwater shoreline as in a saline habitat. So not only should you check the distribution maps but you should also look carefully at the description of the species' normal habitat. Some birds are gradually changing their habitat in a rather subtle way. Up to a few years ago, you hardly ever found a Reed Bunting away from the vicinity of water but recently it seems to be spreading over to drier habitats that are more characteristic of the Yellowhammer.

Jizz

Finally when talking about the different features by which you identify a bird you may hear people saying that it has the 'jizz' of some particular bird. There is nothing magic about the word, which is most often used when you can only see the bird imperfectly against the light or amongst vegetation. Your accumulated experience with birds takes into account what little you can see of its shape and in its method of moving, as well as its habitat and comes up with the impression that the bird is whatever you think it has the 'jizz' of.

Song and calls

Songs, calls or other sounds made by birds such as the drumming of woodpeckers or Snipe are usually a great help to identification. They are often very distinctive. Indeed, it is easier to separate the Chiffchaff and Willow Warbler, Marsh and Willow Tit by their song rather than relying on a distant view. On the other hand, the songs of at least two pairs of birds are difficult to separate, they are the Garden Warbler and the Blackcap, which often sing in similar woodland habitats, and also the Sedge and Reed Warblers, in marshes, and if you happen to be on the Continent or even in some parts of western England you may have the Marsh Warbler to add to the confusion. However, with practice it is possible to sort out most of these problems. Each species has its own vocabulary of call notes by which it communicates to other members of its own species, and sometimes with individuals of similar but different species. The calls of closely related species can be very similar and need a lot of learning. The communication calls of feeding flocks of tits takes a bit of disentangling, as do the 'tacs', 'tecs' and

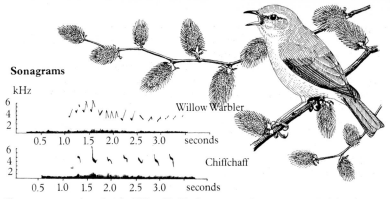

Sonagrams

kHz

6
4
2

Willow Warbler

0.5 1.0 1.5 2.0 2.5 3.0 seconds

6
4
2

Chiffchaff

0.5 1.0 1.5 2.0 2.5 3.0 seconds

These sonagrams show that the Willow Warbler has a greater frequency range and that the pitch of the song descends compared with that of the Chiffchaff. (Sonagrams after Jellis.)

'tucs' of the Garden Warblers, Blackcaps, Whitethroat, Lesser Whitethroats and a host of other warblers.

Like everything else, you learn the song by listening to a strange call in the field, then tracking down the unknown singer and identifying it visually. I also need to write down from time to time a description of the calls or songs.

Some noises produced by birds are not vocalizations at all, for instance, the drumming of the Great and Lesser Spotted Woodpecker when they hammer with their bills on an especially selected piece of a tree, or the drumming of a Snipe as it flies over its breeding habitat, climbing and diving with its tail fanned in such a way that the air rushes past the outer tail feather to produce the bleating sound. When flying over its territory in spring, the Lapwing can create a regular, low-pitched vibrant sound by making an especially hard downward thrust of its wings, which forces the air through the wing feathers. The 'wing-music' of the Mute Swan is well known to all who have been standing round the edge of a lake as a pair has flown past.

The sounds of birds are immensely varied and describing them adequately is a problem. Some like Chiffchaffs, the tits, Yellowhammers and so on, have phrases for which it is relatively simple to produce an alliteration. Others like Blackbirds, Skylarks and warblers, have songs which we now know from the sound spectogram are composed of a series of phrases which may be put together by the singer as it pleases. Other 'songs' are so explosive or gutteral that it is virtually impossible to reproduce them in a written form.

Names of birds

So far when I have referred to a bird I have given it its English name, but I have not explained what a 'species' is or indeed the need for Latin or scientific names. As birdwatchers, we are chiefly interested in species, whether it is a Robin, which has the Latin name or scientific name of *Erithacus rubecula*, or a Great Tit with its scientific name *Parus major*. A species is a population or group which can interbreed and produce fertile offspring. If a member of one

25

Left The experienced birdwatcher discovers birds quickly because he knows the shapes to look for, and it is probably by looking for bird shapes that you will discover two cryptically coloured Nightjars in the centre of this picture (and perhaps a third in the foreground).

Right A woodland habitat can shelter large numbers of birds in the different stratas of vegetation. It is a difficult area to census and usually sample areas are chosen.

Below The largest seabird colonies tend to be in the north where there is abundant fish and where differential erosion has created masses of ledges from horizontal bedding planes of sedimentary rocks.

Two of the Guillemots in the picture are the 'bridled' form with their white 'spectacles'; these have been found to be more common in the more northerly colonies. Although they differ slightly from ordinary Guillemots, they belong to the same species and can interbreed.

species attempted to breed with a member of another species it would generally fail unless the two species were very closely related; if they did succeed in mating then any offspring they produced would be infertile. The species is something real. It is a definite biological unit, which is committed to its own line of evolution. Taxonomists have grouped together species which they think have similar appearances and characteristics into what is known as a 'genus' (plural 'genera') but this grouping is purely subjective.

Linnaeus, a Swedish zoologist, devized a system of naming animals in his *Systema Naturae* in 1758. It is known as the binomial system, every species is placed in a genus and the scientific name of the species thereafter consists both of the generic and the specific names. Hence when I refer to the scientific name of the Blackbird and Song Thrush as *Turdus merula* and *Turdus philomelos* I am also indicating that those birds have been put in the same genus, *Turdus*, with the specific names of *merula* and *philomelos*.

Above the level of species and genus again taxonomists tend to differ over certain points. There are many divisions and sub-divisions, but here I will only mention three: family, order and class. A family is a grouping of genera which taxonomists expect to have evolved from the same parent stem. For instance, the family Fringillidae includes not only finches like the Chaffinch and Linnet but also the Crossbill. An order is a much broader division within the class. The aim of an order is to express the relationship between families of a similar origin. The families Corvidae (crows), Paridae (tits) and Emberizidae (buntings) are all part of the order Passeriformes. Finally, all birds belong to the class Aves.

In the field

Stalking birds

I have emphasized that if you want to get close to birds or if you want them to come close to you, you must behave like a hunter but without his desire to kill. Your subdued clothing will disguise you, and a peaked or brimmed hat will hide the paleness of your face. Thus equipped, you must match your clothing. When you move, your actions should be slow and quiet. If you are with a companion it is best not to talk but if you must, it is better to keep a low voice rather than whisper as sibilant sounds often carry well. When moving, it is best to keep your arms still and, even when you bring your binoculars up to your eyes, be patient and slow if possible, because a hasty movement will disturb what you are looking at. If the bird has already flown or has already seen you and is flying away then you must move fast, remembering, however, that you may disturb something else. The clothes you have chosen should be made of a material that does not rustle as you move about. When walking through a wood avoid treading on sticks that will snap noisily. Old twigs will not always snap if you put your weight on them gently. The quiet approach and then a wait in cover giving a reasonable view may give the best results. If you let the birds treat you as part of the scenery they will come closer.

It is a good idea to arrange your binoculars and field notebook in such a position that they can be used without too much movement. If you are in a wood you should sit or stand with your back to a tree or behind a thinly-leaved bush which can be seen through – it is better to look through such a bush than over the top. If you are on open ground and intend to use a low hedge or bush for cover never look over the top but try to look through them or creep slowly round to the front – hopefully your clothes will blend in sufficiently for the birds not to notice you. If you are walking along the top of a sea or river wall you will be outlined starkly against the sky and will frighten the shy waterfowl and waders for a good distance around. It is better to walk along the wall bottom, which unfortunately is often muddy, and crawl up the bank on your belly and peer carefully between the stems of tall plants along the top. However, if this alternative appears rather daunting, walking along the 'bird-side' of the bank is better than along the top.

Try to make use of any cover as you approach the bird, remembering that if you can see the birds they can see you. If you are careful and cunning you may be able to deceive them for a time but watch their reactions as you approach; ducks' heads may go up to watch you, the nearest may fly away

Above When a bird, like this immature Gannet, is landing the wings are brought forward in a braking action and the primaries are bent back by the resistance of the air. Feet also help with the braking action.

Below The Goldfinch is adapted to extracting the seeds of composite plants from their corollas. Its short legs enable it to hang on to precarious perches and its thin bill enables it to probe into tube-like flowers.

Above The slow wingbeats of the Lapwing and its rounded black and white wings are unmistakable, and a distant flock in the evening light seems to be emitting a pulsating white light.

Below The Grey Wagtail is the typical wagtail of the upland streams in the British Isles. On water meadows in the lowlands its place is taken by the Yellow Wagtail.

and take others with them. If they are satisfied that you present no danger, they will drop their heads and go on feeding or loafing. If you want to try a second approach remember that the birds will already be aware of your presence and therefore much more alert. Small waders may not show much head movement and may simply run ahead of you when you come too close. In many small birds the first sign of anxiety is shown by raising the head, moving the wings out of the breast feathers and an increase in the rate of calling.

Field behaviour

Field behaviour is one aspect of birdwatching in which some people can be rather weak. Two points must always be remembered: firstly, most land, even the foreshore, belongs to someone; secondly, it is important to show a deep concern for the welfare of the birds. Unless you happen to know that a landowner does not object to the public entering his land such as, for instance, the Crown Commissioners who are responsible for the foreshore, you should get permission to enter.

Rights of way throughout the country are very good when local authorities keep them clear, and they enable people to pass and repass through a wide variety of private lands. A map showing rights of way can usually be seen at the County Surveyor's office. You can copy them onto your own Ordnance Survey map as the paths shown on this are not necessarily rights of way.

A number of different codes of conduct have been drawn up for people visiting the country. Most elements of the codes are common sense but it does us all good periodically to think whether in one respect or another we have been thoughtless and so I will repeat here the Countryside Commission's Country Code:—*Guard against all fire risks. Fasten all gates. Keep dogs under proper control. Keep to paths across farmland. Avoid damage to fences, hedges and walls. Leave no litter. Safeguard water supplies. Protect wildlife, wild plants and trees. Go carefully on country roads. Respect the life of the country.* The warning to respect the life of the country is needed, particularly in relation to trespass and sometimes in relation to damage to private property. Also, there have been a number of instances where rare birds have been harried by over-keen listers who have put their own private gratification before the welfare of the bird.

The Wildlife and Country Act 1981 is really a code of conduct for all those who are interested in birds. The theme of the Act is that all wild birds and their nests and eggs are protected. Anything which physically harms them or their nests, eggs or young is forbidden. Some species which are particularly endangered in this country are given special protection, and if anyone commits an offence in respect of them, they are liable to penalties of up to £1000 for each offence. For offences against commoner birds they are liable to maximum fines of £200. Game birds like some of the ducks, pheasants and partridges may be shot in the open season which usually begins in the early autumn and ends before birds begin breeding. There is evidence that certain species like Woodpigeons, House Sparrows and even the beautiful

Bullfinches, in the south-east of England, can be pests and a section in the Act allows authorized people to shoot these species and others listed on the Second Schedule to the Act. The RSPB will send you a copy of their leaflet *Wild Birds and the Law* free of charge if you send them a stamped addressed envelope.

The RSPB's *Birdwatcher's Code* begins with the words: 'The welfare of the birds and its nest should be your first consideration', and this thought should be with you all the time. The BTO produces at least two codes of conduct, one for ringing and one for those who take part in its nest record scheme. The RSPB and the Zoological Photographic Society has published a code of conduct for bird photographers. Each code emphasizes that 'the bird's interest must come first' and then deals with the more practical damage that carelessness on the part of people ringing, nest recording or photographing can do.

A bird's nest is one of the most sensitive places in its life and it is the centre of attraction for many birdwatchers. Some may wish to find nests because they enjoy the search. Others will be recording data for the nest record scheme of the BTO. Bird ringers want to find nests because they wish to ring young so that they may later be able to calculate the ages of the birds more exactly and so follow their lives through. Some may be carrying out life-history studies and the nest is where life begins. There are other people who still collect birds' eggs even though it has long been forbidden by law. Constant examination of the nest can also put it at risk either by causing the bird to desert or by destroying the natural cover or even by making a track to the nest, which predators can easily follow.

Where to see birds
Birds can be found everywhere from city centres and industrial areas to the most luxuriant and ancient woodlands and reedy marshlands. Some can be very obvious like the Blackbirds and Robins in your garden, although both can be very inconspicuous at some times of the year when in woodlands. Some warblers skulk in the bottoms of bushes and reedbeds, occasionally calling to each other, keeping an eye on you, but at the same time being extremely difficult to see. The phrase, 'keeping an eye on you' is a very telling one because when you do manage to catch a sight of the bird it is often the eye that you see, peering at you through some gap in the foliage. Quite a number of birds play hide and seek with you in this way: the Great Spotted Woodpecker hides its body and peers out from behind a tree, while the Wheatear peers over the top of a rock.

Although birds live in almost every habitat the problem is often to find them. The beginner will have difficulty in picking out the same number of birds as the experienced birdwatcher and will wonder at the latter's quickness, which can be despairing at times. Improving the sharpness of your eye is a matter of continual practice. By all means start out with an expert, who will pick out the bird for you, pointing out its shape as it preens or hunts against its natural background. What you are really trying to do at this stage is to learn the shape of all the different species you are likely to see, to learn the 'bird image' in a wide variety of backgrounds, so that you will not think for long that a knob on the branch of a gnarled old tree, or that an oddly shaped tuft of grass on the meadow or a rock on a hillside, is really a bird. Like almost everything else continual practice at searching will bring you the acuity to pick up the 'bird image' whether it is stationary or moving.

How you look at birds will depend to some extent on whether you are walking through the countryside or just sitting quietly. If you are walking and you see a bird with your naked eye that needs identifying you will stop and look at it through your binoculars. However, if you choose a reasonably comfortable position and sit still preferably with the light and some cover behind you, you can sweep large vistas. If you are facing open ground, you can count Lapwings and Golden Plovers, or check the edge of a reed marsh for Herons, Coots and Moorhens or even the stealthy emergence of a Bittern. If you are by an estuary such a position is ideal for counting ducks and waders.

There are many exciting habitats throughout the British Isles and abroad but birdwatcher-naturalists will find, in the long run, that their own 'patch' provides the most rewarding field of discovery. Even living in towns is not a bar to birdwatching and many birdwatchers spend their weekends studying the distribution of birds in the parks and squares. Greater London in particular has some remarkably good birdwatching areas in which much research has been done. The London Natural History Society like many of its kind has a good ornithological section and some of the results of the research are published in its journal the *London Naturalist. The Atlas of Breeding Birds of the London Area* edited by David Montier is also very helpful.

Should you require a change from your own area or, perhaps, when you are on holiday, you will wish to know the best places to look for birds. John Gooders' *Where to Watch Birds* will help you in Britain. This book, as well as giving general guidance, pinpoints reserves, and tells you whether permits are needed.

While most nature reserves are areas of natural or semi-natural vegetation, the Wildfowl Trust specializes in collections of birds. At Slimbridge, Gloucestershire and Peakirk, Northamptonshire, you can see captive wildfowl at close quarters under very good conditions, which may help you solve identification problems. It has also recently been acquiring land as wildfowl refuges where waterfowl may be seen under much wilder conditions.

Your enjoyment of birds on your visits to these areas may be limited to just identifying and listing the birds you have seen. However, my pleasure has been much increased if I have been able to write up a fairly complete description of what I have seen on the visit. From geological maps you can discover the nature of the underlying rock and perhaps details about the soil. A description of the vegetation including the trees, the shrubs and the herb layer, as well as the amount of water present, is useful. This will complement your notes on the bird life and if nothing else the complete description will be much more interesting if you return in later years. If you visit the place

The RSPB protects bird communities in a
wide variety of habitats which are managed
on scientific advice to provide the optimum
conditions for birds.

Ramna Stacks
Fetlar
Yell Sound Islands
Loch of Spiggie

North Hill/Papa Westray
Noup Cliffs
Marwick Head
Birsay Moors and Cottasgarth
North Hoy
Copinsay
Hobbister

Handa
Priest Island
Isle Martin
Culbin Sands
Loch of Strathbeg
Balranald

Loch Garten
Insh Marshes
Killiecrankie
Fowlsheugh
Loch of Kinnordy
Vane Farm
Skinflats
Forth Islands
Loch Grunnart
Inchmickery
Rathlin Island Cliffs
Barnshaugh
Inner Clyde
Horse Island
Lochwinnoch
Wood of Cree
Loch Foyle
Swan Island
Loch Ken/River Dee
Coquet Island
Shanes Castle
Mull of Galloway
Geltsdale
Cowpen Marsh
Castle Caldwell
St Bees Head
Green and Blockhouse Islands
Leighton Moss
and Morecambe Bay
Bempton Cliffs
Hornsea Mere
Gayton Sands
Blacktoft Sands
South Stack
Cliffs
Fairburn Ings
Tetney Marshes
The Skerries
Point of Air
East Wood
Titchwell
Coombes Valley
Lake Vyrnwy
Nene Washes
Snettisham
Mawddach Woods
Strumpshaw Fen
Ynys-hir
Ouse Washes
Minsmere
Gwenffrwd and Dinas
Fowlmere
North Warren
The Lodge and Sutton Fen
Wolves Wood
Nagshead
Stour Wood
Grassholm
Rye House Marsh
Havergate
Church Wood
Island
Hedgerley
Chapel Wood
Northward Hill
Barfold Copse
Elmley Marshes
West Sedgemoor
Langstone Harbour
Forewood
Aylesbeare
Arne
Dungeness
Radipole Lake
Church Wood, Blean

A view across the valley of the Doethie to the Sessile Oak woods of the RSPB's reserve at the Gwenffrwd where Pied Flycatchers, Redstarts and Wood Warblers nest. Kites may occasionally forage over the sheep walks.

regularly over the years your notes may provide a basis for a history of vegetation and bird population changes.

When to see birds

Birds are present in almost any type of habitat throughout the year. Seasonally, their abundance may well vary and these changes should be of interest to the birdwatcher-naturalist. He will want to know why birds are absent or why there has been a change, so even an empty habitat is not devoid of interest.

In the 'bird-year' the seasons seem to merge imperceptively into each other. For instance, spring begins in March but many birds have already established their nesting territories by then. Our familiar Robin, for example, has probably been singing since January or even late December. Early spring is a good time to search for birds as the swelling leaf buds do not yet make an effective barrier. It is now that you should watch out for the first Chiffchaffs, while they search continuously for early insects amongst the taller deciduous trees. On the days immediately after their arrival they will sing a quiet subsong which is very different from their usual song which for many birdwatchers is the first sign that our summer migrants are on their way. Shortly after the arrival of the Chiffchaff, the Willow Warbler can be heard sometimes singing in the same trees as the former bird, but also from the lower shrub layer.

On the coastal cliffs and shingle banks and the bare heavily grazed links and dunes, the first Wheatears will have begun to appear. Arriving earliest on the westernmost peninsulas of Cornwall and Wales, they seem to penetrate through to the eastern parts of England a week or so later. In Dyfed the first large influx appears to average about the 29th of March, although the first birds might have arrived three weeks earlier.

Along the laneside hedges and gardens birds are returning from their winter wandering to nest. By mid-March the first Greenfinches and Linnets are beginning to settle down. These birds are largely absent during the winter, appearing at the bird table only after cold weather or a snowfall. Our Goldfinches, which winter south of Britain, arrive later in April, and nest in the old pear and apple trees which are no longer pruned or sprayed.

On the islands and seabird cliffs the auks come and go. Guillemots may have visited the ledges for brief periods from November onwards and now in late March and early April they have been joined by Razorbills and Puffins and sit, bobbing about, on the sea. Then early one morning the Razorbills and Guillemots paddle rapidly over the water, lift off and circle upwards and in towards the cliffs, landing finally with a thump on their ledges. Usually the Puffins remain on the water until around midday when the two other species are going to sea again. Suddenly thousands of these clown-like birds will circle up over the clifftops. Some return to the sea again but others alight and either rush at once into a burrow or stand on the sward, waddling around, peering into others' burrows. Masses of them, too, just circle overhead.

In April and May the later migrants arrive and establish their breeding territories. Others are passing on to their breeding grounds further north. Birds seeking shelter for their nests and food for their young gradually return to habitats which have been empty throughout the winter. On the other hand, estuaries which have been teeming with bird-life during the winter months are now empty as there is nowhere for the birds to breed. During June the last of the summer migrants will have arrived and those which have been successful in obtaining mates will be well on with their nesting. By now the young of the first Wheatears to arrive will be leaving their nests and from then on the numbers of young birds launching themselves into the world will be increasing enormously. May and June are wonderful months to travel in Britain whether it is to the mountains and moorlands, or to the sea with its cliffs and islands or to the northern forests and lakes. The island cliffs are beautiful with their huge drifts of Sea Campion, Thrift and the occasional Spring Squill.

As summer creeps up the hills many species of bird such as the Skylark, Meadow Pipit, Wheatear, Curlew and Golden Plover, together with the occasional Dunlin, can be found nesting among the heather, rushes, sedge and bog cotton. On the Orkney moors the Arctic Skuas, Common Gulls and even the Great Skua have come to nest.

By mid-June the breeding season has finished for some species. Some of the waders have failed to find mates or have lost their eggs or young and from this time onwards small flocks of Lapwings can be seen dispersing as they fly across England towards Wales, or even Ireland. In the arable counties of England the cereal crop has not been harvested and there are few places for the Lapwing to rest. In Cambridgeshire, the Lapwing numbers build up after the harvest, when the ground has been ploughed or burned. The Curlews also move west, but in much smaller numbers, at this time. The Green Sandpiper appears in smaller numbers still and can be found, interestingly, foraging along the edges of quite small streams and ponds, even in gardens.

In July some of the earlier migrants are already beginning their return journeys. The bulk of the Swifts leave after a short breeding season. In the woods the singing has stopped and the thick foliage make birds difficult to find. It is also the time of year when birds are difficult to identify too. Many of the drakes are in eclipse plumage and look like the ducks and as a result of losing their flight feathers are barely able to fly. The juvenile plumages of many like Starlings, Robins and gulls, for example, are sufficiently different from the adult plumage to be confusing.

August is the 'betwixt and between' month, the first half of which is not particularly good for birds. Most of them have finished breeding, the adults are moulting and their young have dispersed from their nesting sites, some are also busy fattening themselves up in readiness for their long and sometimes hazardous journey to their winter quarters. Channel Islanders may see a large movement of small warblers from the 20th to the 25th of August. Also in the last half of August such birds as the Dunlin, Turnstone, Ringed Plover, Redshank and Curlew begin to re-appear in large numbers on our shores. Some will move on but a few will be staying with us. This is the season for change: birds are moving from one part of the world to another and from one habitat to another. Some of the most noticeable visible migration is provided by the Swallows moving south along the coast towards the shortest sea crossing in the southeast.

Later in the autumn, the movement can become spectacular when the Swallows are joined by Meadow Pipits, Starlings, Lapwings, Chaffinches and Bramblings, all tending to move in a roughly westerly or south-westerly direction but occasionally being directed away from their main course by some geographical feature. The observation of visible migration has tended to become a little unfashionable because the use of radar techniques has solved so many problems. However, in order to experience the pure thrill of birds, there is nothing like the rush of migrants an hour or so after sunrise on a calm bright morning. Although you can see large numbers migrating in some parts of Britain, the spectacular movements take place on the continent.

Many species migrate at night and radar is needed to detect their direction of flight and the times of the movement. Redwings, Fieldfares and other thrushes which move at night often reveal their presence as they fly over by their calls.

Finally, during winter from December to March, most birds have left their breeding habitats to find the places where food is more abundant. The moorlands and cliffs are now empty while the estuaries are full of birds, and some fields, particularly those that are grazed by sheep, now hold masses of Lapwings and Golden Plover and various species of thrush. Fields, hedges, rick yards and even small wooded villages with mature gardens which have the aspect of rather open woodland, can support large numbers of birds, although the woods themselves hold fewer birds in winter. Strangers from the far north may winter here, such as the Rough-legged Buzzard, the Great Grey Shrike and northern duck like the Smew and Long-tailed Duck appear around our coast.

If the weather should harden and snow and ice come in from the east you may see spectacular foul-weather movements with thousands of birds heading west, and in the west itself you may see them leaving the headlands of Dyfed to cross the sea to Ireland.

January and February can be cold and harsh but after the mid-winter solstice the Robin and the Skylark begin to sing again. During the following months they are joined by other hedgerow birds bringing us back to March and the beginning of spring.

Counting birds

In order to study many of the different aspects of the lives of birds we have to count them. Counting can tell us how many birds make use of the whole or part of a habitat for such activities as feeding, nesting or roosting. Regular counts can show us if there are changes in numbers and, if this is the case, it may become important to discover the reasons. They could be seasonal, with some individuals migrating over long distances, some only a few kilometres, and other species from harsher climates coming to take their place. Counting by birdwatchers has in recent years shown that often changes have resulted from habitat destruction and environmental hazards, such as organo-chlorine pesticides, oil pollution and even, though it was thousands of kilometres away, the effect which a disastrous drought in the Sahel Region had on the European bird populations which wintered there.

Counting birds is by no means easy. In some places, for instance, a small lake, you can see all the birds quite clearly but in a wood of the same size this is quite impossible. Birds and their habitats are so variable that different methods of counting are required for each of them. To make things more difficult there is no agreement as to the ideal method of counting. It is also difficult to be certain that one person's figures are comparable to another's, even when working in the same area.

Counts are either direct or based on some form of estimation. In a direct count you must be able to see each individual bird. This method is suitable for lakes, estuaries, seabird cliffs, open fields and small flocks of birds in flight or at sea. If you cannot see all the birds at once, for instance, in a woodland habitat or when counting a very large and fast-flying flock, you should count one or more samples and calculate the total from those figures.

Direct counts A direct count should produce a more exact figure as, with a small lake, you can see all the birds at once. If the lake is large, however, you can run into problems as a substantial portion of a flock might move to a part of the lake as yet uncounted. Nevertheless, regular counts of lakes can be very useful. The results may be of value to the wildfowl counts which are organized in this country by the Wildfowl Trust, as well as by local county bird clubs. It is also worth counting any small area which can be seen easily,

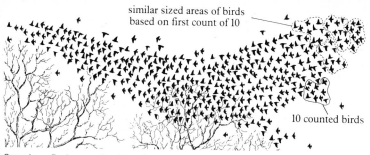

similar sized areas of birds based on first count of 10

10 counted birds

Some large flocks move too fast to be counted accurately. Count a group of ten or a hundred and estimate the number of tens or hundreds there are in the flock.

such as a pasture, field or estuary, especially if you visit it regularly. Over the years the results could show interesting changes.

Estimated counts The second method of arriving at a total number when counting birds is by estimating. This is done when direct counting is difficult or impossible due to the numbers of birds or the habitat. The operation almost invariably falls into two parts: firstly, a direct count of one or more samples is made and, secondly, a division of the flock is carried out using the size of the sample as the basic unit. For example, first count part of the flock, say ten birds, and then estimate how many groups of ten there are in the flock. The flock might be so large that the estimate will be in thousands. In order to account for any error an estimate of the largest and smallest size that the flock might be, should be given. Plenty of practice is needed and a useful aid to precision can be obtained if you photograph the flock and count the birds at leisure later and then compare this figure with your original estimate. Another problem for the unwary is that some birdwatchers tend to over-estimate the numbers of large birds and under-estimate the number of small birds. Whenever possible, it is a good idea to compare your counts with other people's.

Exactly the same principle of estimating is used when you are counting the number of birds in any habitat. Several methods may be used. In the breeding season you can attempt to locate all the nests in a part of a habitat but this is very time consuming and more often it is better to locate the singing males on the supposition that they are holding territory and are probably nesting. To obtain an estimate for the whole of a habitat, which should have approximately the same ecological structure, you census one or more sample areas and arrive at an average for the different species within the area. Then a calculation of the total size of the population is made by multiplying the population of sample area by the number of times that the total area is divisible by this sample area. For instance, the sample area may cover 8 hectares (20 acres) and the total area may be 80 hectares (200 acres). The total number of pairs of Blue Tits in the sample area may be 9, therefore there will be approximately $\frac{80}{8} \times 9 = 90$ pairs. This system is commonly used for estimating game populations in the USA and some other countries.

Common Birds Census The Common Birds Census was started in 1961. It is organized by the BTO and is the most satisfactory system for measuring bird populations, at present. If you wish to undertake a Common Birds Census in your area, you should get the full details from the BTO at Tring. Basically you select a study area ranging in size from approximately 20–25 hectares with woodland habitat to 80 hectares in open country such as farmland. You need to make eight or more visits lasting several hours, before the end of the summer. To have any value you must be prepared to carry this on over several seasons; continuity of record is most important. If you are working through the BTO 1:2500 outline maps will be provided free of charge.

Line transect method While the Common Birds Census is the most precise method of measuring bird populations it is also somewhat time consuming and complicated. There are two further methods of sampling, which are simpler to use, although they forfeit some precision. The first of these methods is the line transect which is and has been used by people sampling a wide range of habitats in a number of different countries. This also has the advantage over the Common Birds Census in that it can be used throughout the year, enabling you to measure winter populations.

On a line transect you walk through your chosen habitat along a regular path and record all the birds you identify either by sight or sound. You do not need to map their positions, although it is better if you do. There are, however, various conventions which you should observe. Most observers

During my survey of Hayley Wood in Cambridgeshire, I recorded all the birds seen or heard within 25m (80ft) of a line transect which passed through the different woodland habitats.

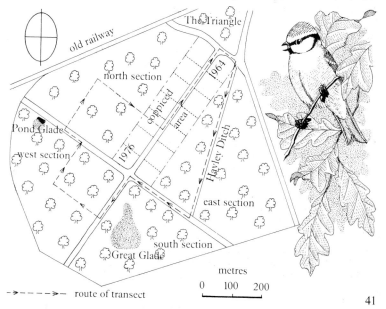

route of transect

seem to recommend an average speed of about 3 km (2 miles) an hour. Also you count all birds within 25 m (80 ft) of the line. Some birds are more conspicuous than others and so it is difficult to compare results between one species and another or for one species from one wood to another, except where the birds are conspicuous. Nevertheless, the system can be quite useful for comparing a number of singing passerines.

From the figures resulting from the line transect, which is in effect a sample census, you can derive a rough estimate of the total number of birds in the wood. Furthermore, if you continue to make line transects throughout the year you can detect seasonal and annual variations in the bird populations.

When I am travelling and I have to move faster than a line transect allows, whether on foot or some form of transport such as a boat, I keep a fifteen minute check-list of the birds observed. Normally I use squared paper in my notebook, listing the birds on the left-hand side and using a column for each fifteen minutes. I use a 'tick' to record a sighting, or a figure, if I have counted, with an additional symbol for a song, nesting, etc. This can give some indication of the distribution of birds over a large area. If you can also add notes about the types of habitats through which you are passing, the record will be that much more valuable.

Spot census This is another sampling method which lacks many of the good qualities of the Common Birds Census, but it can be used throughout the year and is good for assessing the relative abundance of birds in different habitats. Spot censuses can be made in a number of ways. For instance, take ten points which are roughly the same distance from each other and which are easily identified. Wait for five minutes recording all the birds which can be seen or heard within a 25m (80ft) radius.

Counting cliff-nesting birds The counting of seabirds on nesting cliffs in large colonies can be very difficult and, for the fool-hardy, dangerous. It might be quite simple to count the number of individual birds on some cliffs, but that figure does not tell you the numbers that are really nesting there, for you cannot always see the eggs or young birds and the number of seabirds visiting the colony may vary considerably throughout the day.

It is not always possible to see from one point the whole of a very extensive tern or gull colony on flat ground. In these colonies it is possible to count a sample area and estimate the total from this. However, these colonies should not be disturbed unless it is for an important scientific reason and then only by an ornithologist who knows what he is doing.

Counting birds on cliffs poses yet more problems. Unless it is a very small colony you will probably not be able to see all the birds at once. You, therefore, have to move your position to get a new angle on the colony and have the added difficulty of determining whether you are looking at the edge of the section you have just counted, or, indeed, whether you have missed some. Counting from a boat is not easy since, more often than not, it moves up and down! Photography of a cliff from a boat or land and then a later count can help too, but, if you have a mixed colony, identification of all the birds can be an extremely difficult task.

The structure of birds

Anatomy

The structure of most birds is related to their ability to fly and this imposes a number of restrictions on their bone structure and body shape. Because a bird can fly it is desirable that its bones should not only be strong but also light. To achieve this some bones have air spaces or cavities which are crossed by bony struts to strengthen them. These cavities are particularly well developed in large gliding and soaring birds such as vultures, albatrosses and eagles but are less so in diving birds such as ducks and cormorants, presumably because any additional buoyancy would require extra energy on the part of the bird when it wanted to dive. Some of the bones have also been strengthened during the course of evolution by the fusion of many of the bones of their reptilian ancestors. On the other hand, the flexibility of the neck has been increased by the large number of vertebrae, ranging from thirteen in the Cuckoo and other song birds to as many as twenty-eight in the swan. This gives the bird freedom to move its head while searching for food, watching for enemies, preening and so on.

The upper and lower mandibles (the bill) are a bony adaptation of the skull which are covered with a horny sheath. The shape of the bill is usually adapted to a bird's feeding behaviour, but occasionally as with Puffins and herons the formation of the bill plays an important part in the bird's displays. Flesh-eating species such as hawks, owls, shrikes and even the fish-eating shearwaters have hooked bills for tearing their prey. Some waders such as Snipe have long thin bills which they use for probing deeply into the mud; the tip is sensitive so that they can detect their prey. Nightjars on the other hand have short, but very wide bills, which enable them to catch flying insects more easily. Even among the finches there is a variety of shapes and sizes, from the Goldfinch's long and thin bill, which is used for poking into Teazel florets, to the twisted bill of the Crossbill, which is used for extracting seed from conifer cones. Birds do not have real teeth although several species have appendages which have the appearance of teeth.

Legs and toes vary enormously. The four toes are arranged in a variety of ways depending on how the bird obtains its food. In most perching birds three toes point forward and one points to the rear. This arrangement suits best the way of life which involves perching on branches and twigs. Woodpeckers which cling to the sides of trees have two claws pointing forwards and two backwards, one of which they can move forwards.

Different shapes of bill

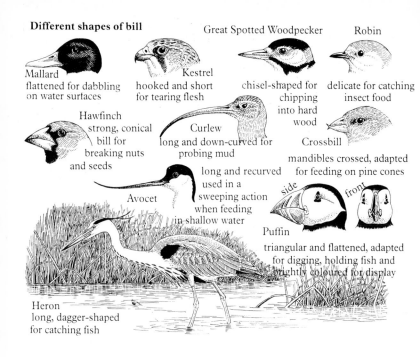

Mallard
flattened for dabbling on water surfaces

Kestrel
hooked and short for tearing flesh

Great Spotted Woodpecker
chisel-shaped for chipping into hard wood

Robin
delicate for catching insect food

Hawfinch
strong, conical bill for breaking nuts and seeds

Curlew
long and down-curved for probing mud

Crossbill
mandibles crossed, adapted for feeding on pine cones

Avocet
long and recurved used in a sweeping action when feeding in shallow water

Puffin
side   front
triangular and flattened, adapted for digging, holding fish and brightly coloured for display

Heron
long, dagger-shaped for catching fish

The bills of birds are adapted to their feeding and sometimes to their courtship requirements.

Flight

In flapping flight (rather than gliding), forward propulsion is provided mainly by the wing tips or the primaries and the chief function of the secondary feathers is to give lift – they move relatively little as the wing beats. On the down beat the wings move powerfully not only downwards but forwards with the feathers closed. The flight feathers are flexible and twist like a propeller so that the downward movement pulls the bird through the air. On the upstroke, which also drives the bird through the air although fractionally less powerfully, the primaries open like a venetian blind to allow the air through. The bird rotates its wings at the shoulder to increase the angle of attack in order to maintain lift and once again the primaries are bent on the upstroke. If a bird wishes to alter course it can do so by tilting its body or adjusting its wings and tail.

Taking-off can be difficult for birds. Swans have to run to attain the necessary air speed, auks need a vertical cliff to jump off, while others like some of the vultures have difficulty raising themselves from the ground unless it is sufficiently heated to provide strong thermals. Passerines on the other hand can take-off simply by jumping into the air. They obtain the forward thrust they need by flicking their wings backwards during the upstroke and obtain the required lift by using a powerful downstroke.

Once in the air a bird can glide without beating its wings for various lengths of time depending upon the shape of the wings and the body length. Some birds, like the gulls and albatrosses, are able to glide rapidly, while slower gliding birds such as the broad-winged hawks and vultures tend to lose height more slowly. Many birds are able to soar making use of up-currents. Fulmars and gulls make use of these along cliffs; petrels and shearwaters glide along ocean waves; buzzards use the rising currents over hills and vultures and many other species use the warm thermals. Some birds can hover by reducing their speed to that of the wind but real hovering birds such as Kestrels and terns have to take a nearly vertical stance and beat their wings backwards and forwards in a horizontal plane.

Feather structure

Feathers are of two main types; firstly, there are the flight and contour feathers which give the bird its shape and provide outer insulation. Secondly, there are the down feathers which are found beneath the contour feathers and

The skeleton of a bird must provide a strong but light framework. Hollow bones with cross-struts help reduce weight yet give adequate strength.

Skeleton of a pigeon

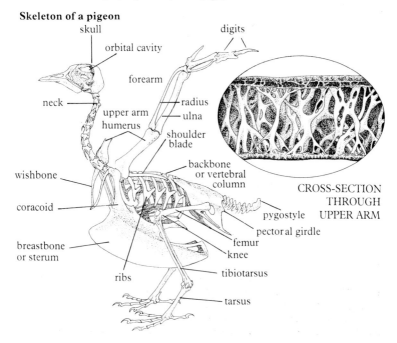

skull
digits
orbital cavity
forearm
neck
radius
upper arm
ulna
humerus
shoulder
blade
backbone
or vertebral
column
wishbone
CROSS-SECTION
THROUGH
UPPER ARM
coracoid
pygostyle
pectoral girdle
breastbone
femur
or sterum
knee
ribs
tibiotarsus
tarsus

45

Different shapes of feet

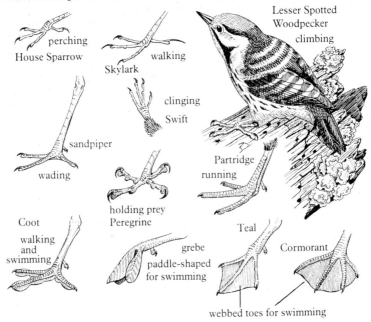

These drawings indicate what a wide variety of legs and claws birds have evolved in response to their various means of locomotion.

provide extra insulation. All other feathers are intermediate between these two. Herons and other waterbirds, as well as some birds of prey have special powder-down feathers which grow continuously and gradually disintegrate into a fine powder which is used in feather maintenance and cleanliness.

Function of feathers
Feathers have many different and important functions: they are used for conserving warmth, for flying, and for protecting the bird against knocks. The colour of the feathers is important for both camouflage and courtship displays. During the winter the contour feathers are fluffed out in order to trap a thick pocket of warm air between the feathers and the skin; conversely on hot days in summer they are ruffled to allow hot air to escape more easily.

Feather colour
Two of the functions of feather colour appear to be contradictory: one is self-advertisement and the other is self-concealment. In many species a balance is

struck between these needs, the male being brightly coloured, especially in the breeding season, and the female being camouflaged by drab coloration. In the Dotterel and the Red-necked Phalarope the normal coloration and roles are reversed and the male, which is more drably coloured, incubates the eggs and looks after the young. In many species their striking colours can be used for both functions depending on the posture the bird adopts. For instance, the black patches of the Wheatear can be used as self-advertisement when the bird is displaying but also helps to disguise it when it is motionless amidst the rocks and stones. Furthermore, self-advertisement has the dual purpose of threatening males or attracting females and thus we find that one colour in a bird can carry several messages.

Feather moult

To be at peak efficiency throughout a bird's life feathers have to be shed and renewed once or twice a year, depending on the species of bird. In almost all species a few feathers are renewed at a time, usually in pairs on either side of the body. The moulting of the wing feathers seriously impairs the ability of a bird to fly and in some cases prevents it from flying altogether. Drakes lose all their flight feathers at once and are therefore flightless for some weeks in late summer, this is when they are said to be in 'eclipse'. However, their marshy habitat at this season of the year usually provides them with adequate food and shelter, and their sober 'eclipse' plumage affords them extra camouflage.

Normally birds do not moult during the breeding season, on migration or during times of food shortage as they need all the energy they can obtain to generate new feathers and to replace heat loss during the moult. However, there are all sorts of odd exceptions. Seabirds moult during the breeding season which is probably because it is safer to moult while they are on land than when they are out at sea. Migratory birds usually moult after the breeding season when there is plenty of food available and before their long flight to their winter quarters. Other species migrate to relatively safe areas to moult, the Shelduck, for example, uses Bridgwater Bay in Somerset and the Eider Duck collects off the coast of Aberdeenshire in July. The Common Scoter gathers in flocks of 150,000 birds in one spot off the Danish coast.

Some birds moult more than once a year. The Ptarmigan moults three times: one complete autumn moult produces its brown plumage, two partial moults produce the white winter plumage and then a third moult gives it the grey spring plumage. The Purple Sandpiper has what is known as an 'arrested' moult which begins in the breeding grounds and then continues in the winter quarters, after migration. This arrested moult may result from the fact that large birds take a long time to moult and cannot afford to wait too long as the summer food supply soon becomes exhausted. This is a particular danger if the birds happen to be insectivorous.

The time taken for moulting and changing feathers varies enormously. Some long distance migrants can lose and replace their feathers within thirty-five days prior to the migration. The Curlew Sandpiper, and the shore waders which moult when they reach their winter quarters can take six or seven months to moult; eagles can take more than a year with several pauses in the change of their plumage.

The bright new feathers of a bird's plumage are not always the result of a spring moult. Sometimes the brightly coloured feathers grow in the autumn but are tipped with a duller colour. In spring the tip is lost by abrasion and the brighter colours are revealed. One obvious example is provided by the black breast of the House Sparrow which is hidden by the grey feather tips in winter.

Feather maintenance

Proper maintenance ensures that the feathers are kept in good condition between moults. Preening is the most important form of maintenance and a bird will spend quite a large proportion of its day pulling feathers through the tip of its bill to clean them and zip up any loose barbs. It will also peck at its feathers to remove foreign matter including feather parasites. The bird will work through the various feather tracts, lifting its wings to peck at the primaries and turning its head through all sorts of angles to get at the rump and tail feathers. It is impossible for a bird to preen its own head so it resorts to scratching it with one foot while balancing on the other. Herons and other fish-eating birds have a special claw to remove fish slime from feathers.

Bathing When there is water available, bathing may often precede the daily routine of feather maintenance. Everyone who has a bird-bath or pond in their garden can watch Blackbirds and other birds regularly having a splash.

Shallow birdbaths can easily be made from an old dustbin lid. Many birds like this thrush dip their heads into the water, swill it over their backs and then splash it with their wings.

48

The reason the Cormorant and to a lesser extent the Shag hang out their wings in this way is still not clear; whether it is to dry out the feathers is still disputed by ornithologists.

The point of bathing is not to wash the feathers so much as to dampen them so that the oiling which follows next is more effective: the washing of feathers and skin seems to be of only secondary importance.

Birds only need to dampen their feathers; if they get them too wet this will affect their ability to fly and is therefore dangerous. Many birds have a 'rain-posture' during which they stand upright with their feathers close to the body so that the rain runs off the plumage quite rapidly.

The most common method of removing the moisture from the feathers is to raise and then depress the contour feathers and at the same time relax and jerk the body forward. Waterbirds, which dry themselves while resting on the water, raise and flap their wings in addition to this movement. Cormorants and Shags leave the water to preen their feathers and can be regularly seen standing on rocks and posts with their wings outstretched; why they should do this is still not clear. Ducks and some gulls also perform special movements in flight to shake water off their feathers; gulls can often be seen shaking their wings and bodies in flight after bathing.

Oiling After bathing and drying a bird may smear oil on to the feathers from the oil gland which is situated just above the rump. The oil gland is largest in some of the seabirds and waterbirds and may be partly related to their aquatic life and help with waterproofing, but it is missing from Woodpeckers and some other species. It may also help to preserve the horny covering of the bill. Furthermore there is some experimental evidence that the secretion applied to the plumage may enable vitamin D to be synthesized under the influence of sunlight and then presumably absorbed either through the skin or ingested in subsequent preening.

A Blackbird sunning. The exact purpose of this activity, which often occurs after preening, oiling, or dusting, is still something of a mystery. In this posture the oil gland at the base of the tail is exposed.

Sunning Several species of birds can be found deliberately exposing their bodies to the sun using a special posture. Some people consider that the posture in which the bird lies on its belly with wings and tail spread widely, is a simple response to temperature. Sometimes, the wings may be raised and feathers twisted round – a position which may vary according to the species. However, even on cool days exposure to the sun changes the chemical quantity of oil from the preen gland, and maybe it is the light rather than the warmth which is biologically important.

Dusting Some species of bird, particularly game birds and others which may have originated from arid areas, dust themselves by driving sand and other fine particles amongst their feathers. They will find a dusty hollow and drive the dust into the feathers either by shuffling themselves or by scratching the dust with their feet, sometimes both the wings and feet are used. House Sparrows frequently dust themselves, perhaps to dislodge or discourage the feather and skin parasites.

Anting In addition to all these methods of feather maintenance some passerines anoint themselves with the body fluid of ants. The bird which I have seen doing this most often is the Starling. The important part of the fluid is formic acid which is produced by some worker ants but fluids from other groups of ants are also used. This probably assists in the care of the feathers as formic acid is known to be an insecticide and may kill or discourage the ectoparasites. Anting is actually carried out by the bird smearing ants with its bill directly on to the feathers or by letting the ants swarm over it and penetrate between the feathers while ejecting their formic acid.

The five senses

Vision This is extremely important to birds and some have an eyesight which is eight times keener than man's. Relatively speaking a Starling's eyeball is fifteen times heavier than a man's; an eagle's eyeball is actually larger than a man's. They are generally so large that there is little room for movement and as a result birds have very flexible necks and most species can rotate their heads through 180°. Birds can also see through a much wider angle as a result of the position of the eye in the head. An owl can see through about 100°, up to 70° of which will be binocular vision, while a pigeon can see through 340°, only a small percentage of which will be binocular. Birds see colour in essentially the same way as human beings but they also have an adaptation which may help to improve their vision in hazy weather. In addition to the normal eyelid birds have a nictitating membrane which acts as a third transparent eyelid and is drawn horizontally across the eye from the nasal-side backwards. It can clean or moisten the surface of the eye without shutting out the light. In many waterbirds, this clear window-like lens is so refractive that it bends the light rays even under water.

Hearing Birds depend on their sense of hearing for keeping in touch with other members of the flock or their family, for hearing alarm calls or in some cases even hearing their prey. Apparently some of the plovers can actually

The Woodcock can watch for possible enemies through 360° which is very necessary when its beak is probing deeply in the ground. Raptors, including the Tawny Owl, have binocular vision which allows them to judge distances more accurately: this is essential for hunting prey. Passerines, including the House Sparrow, are less specialized and their angle of vision is midway between these extremes.

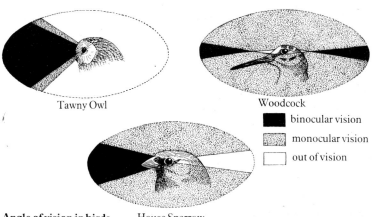

Tawny Owl

Woodcock

■ binocular vision

▨ monocular vision

□ out of vision

Angle of vision in birds   House Sparrow

listen to earthworms; the Barn Owl can apparently locate its prey by sound alone. Although birds have a similar range of hearing to human beings – from 20 to 20,000 cycles per second, they can hear sounds that are too rapid for us to hear and can locate sounds by assessing the time-lag between its arrival at either side of the head. It is also easier to locate the origin of brief sounds rather than long drawn out ones which is probably why the alarm calls for many species are long drawn-out whistles or other sounds.

Smell, taste and touch These senses are of little value to birds since their eyes are so strongly developed. Some species may be able to smell food while it is in their mouth and this ability can cause some birds to spit out food which is tainted or obnoxious, such as ants. Taste and touch are generally poorly developed as well – indeed it is not well known what birds can taste. The sense of touch is much the same as man's. However, birds do have special nerve-endings which appear to be particularly sensitive to vibrations such as the shaking of their perch. Waders have sensitive tips to their beaks which allow them to detect their unseen prey. It is also thought that the rictal bristles around the mouth of flycatchers and Nightjars, which are modified feathers, may not only help the bird to catch food but may also be sensitive to vibrations caused by their prey.

Behaviour

Most behaviour patterns are instinctive and are performed without any preliminary experience or learning. From the moment that a bird in its egg starts to cut its way out, or to stretch up its head in the nest and open its beak, it is acting instinctively. It knows when to migrate, where to migrate to and in the following year how to build a nest and reproduce. All these instincts connected with reproduction, feeding and migration are inherited and whilst this innate behaviour usually serves the bird well, almost all these activities can be improved as the bird learns through experience. Although since the bird has a small brain its capacity to learn is limited. Instinct, therefore, is the inherited or innate tendency to act in a certain way in response to a certain situation. The behaviour pattern is almost as stereotyped and as flexible as is the innate tendency for an animal to be of a certain size, shape or colour. The basic 'themes' of bird song are instinctive. Most young birds react instinctively to the alarm notes of the parents, even when the parent may have different alarm notes for different dangers.

This instinct generally helps the individual to survive; innate behaviour comes from survivors and generally will be passed on further. Innate behaviour usually occurs in somewhat stereotyped patterns which are very constant in form, and are triggered by stimuli around them. For instance, in spring it is fairly easy to see how a Robin's red breast triggers off aggressive activities in other Robins defending their territories. Exposure of the white rump of Bullfinches or the white outer tail feathers of a Chaffinch, trigger off flight in other Bullfinches or Chaffinches feeding close by. The red patch on the Herring Gull's bill will trigger the feeding behaviour pattern of begging for food by a hungry, young bird.

Migration and ringing

Migration

While migration occurs in other animal groups it is most pronounced in birds. Broadly speaking, bird migration is a regular movement between the breeding areas and those which are best suited to feeding needs at other times of the year so that birds are able to exploit food that would otherwise be unavailable. Also young can be reared in areas that provide sufficient food in the appropriate season but which may be very inhospitable at other times of the year. Since most northern species breed during the summer months migration takes place in the spring and autumn.

Most birds are migratory to some degree. There is every gradation between really sedentary species and those like the Arctic Tern, which travels some 18,000km (11,000 miles) from the Arctic Circle to the Antarctic. Some birds may only make a purely local movement during the winter months like the adult Greenfinches which wander around within a few kilometres of where they normally nest, although young Greenfinches can travel several hundred kilometres.

The classic long-distance migrant is the Swallow. It breeds over much of the northern hemisphere and those from temperate Europe winter south of the Sahara in Africa, often retaining their geographical grouping. The British population concentrates on the moist south-east region of South Africa. The timing of the Swallow's arrival in Britain probably depends upon the availability of certain types of flying insects. It is a day-migrant and its movements are so obvious that we can trace them northwards in spring and southwards in autumn from the records which are kept by many people all over Europe. The main direction of the autumn passage of Swallows through Britain lies to the south-east and south – a direction which generally leads them to the shorter Channel sea-crossing and avoids the longer crossing towards Spain. This direction is maintained into Europe, but some apparently turn south or south-west after reaching north France. Like so many other species which winter south of the Sahara or Libyan desert most Swallows cross the thousand or so kilometres of the western Sahara.

On their return northwards, analysis of the Swallow-ringing recoveries indicates that they tend to retrace the path of their autumn migration although the final stages of the spring return may pass further north and east to Belgium and the Netherlands and the final direction of the spring movement into Britain and within Britain is mainly to the north-west and northwards. Sometimes geographical factors can divert these birds from their preferred direction. A study of Swallows and other day migrants in your area could show how local geographical factors affect the direction of their flight.

Many different species of birds such as Redwings and Fieldfares which breed to the north and east of us winter in the British Isles unless the weather is so hard that ice and snow cover the land. Then the birds are forced to fly yet further south and west in search of food. Other species use Britain as a staging post, and many of our estuaries are used in this way by waders from the north. The Barnacle Goose which winters here is interesting in that it has three populations which have quite distinct breeding and wintering areas: the Greenland population winters on the north-west coasts of Scotland and Ireland; the Spitzbergen population winters in the Solway and the Russian population in the Netherlands. There is no evidence of any large-scale mixing, even in their winter quarters which may be as little as 100km (60 miles) apart.

How do the birds which undertake these long migrations know where to go and when they should return? Although orientation and navigation in birds has been much studied recently, the answer is still unclear but it is known that some birds find their way by a form of compass navigation using the position of the sun as a guide.

It is also thought that many of the night migrants can orientate by the stars. Problems arise when stars are obscured in the course of a migratory flight. Radar observations have shown that it is possible for birds to continue on their line even though the stars have been obscured by cloud. If, however, strong winds arise the birds may then become completely disorientated and be blown off course. In autumn, for instance, birds may begin their autumn flight in a south-westerly direction under anti-cyclonic conditions with a clear sky. Should they meet cyclonic conditions with strong winds and overcast skies they may lose all points of reference and drift down wind. It is this sort of drift which often results in the exciting migrants turning up on the coast.

Seabirds, like landbirds, migrate in order to avoid the scarcity of food. Some birds such as gulls, Razorbills and Guillemots, spend most of the winter on the continental shelf, while others like albatrosses and Puffins roam far out to sea. Some species seem to have a fairly definite wintering area but the movement of other species such as Little Auks, and petrels are little known and may be affected by the wind direction and strength.

To take a few examples, Herring Gulls, during the winter, wander locally around the coast of Britain, probably not travelling more than 200–300km (150–200 miles) from their nesting areas. On the east coast the numbers of local birds may be swollen by visitors from north-western Europe. On the other hand the Lesser Black-backed Gull, which is closely related to the Herring Gull, is chiefly a summer visitor to Britain and in winter travels to the western Mediterranean and the Atlantic as well as Europe and Africa as far south as Nigeria.

The most remarkable migration is that of the Arctic Tern. It nests along the

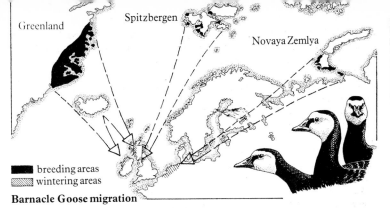

Barnacle Goose migration

The three geographical races of the Barnacle Goose not only breed in different localities but do not even mix when they are in their winter quarters even though they may be less than a hundred kilometres apart.

north coasts of Europe, Asia and North America and spends our winter in the southern Atlantic and in the Pacific and occasionally even below the Antarctic Circle. The American breeding population crosses the Atlantic in autumn before turning south and then moves down the eastern half of the Atlantic, having joined up with the northern European population. Finally, some of these birds reach the Antarctic pack-ice and spread out along its edge.

The migration of the Arctic Tern is one of the longest in the world. Some birds nest within the Arctic Circle and winter within the Antarctic Circle along the edge of the ice.

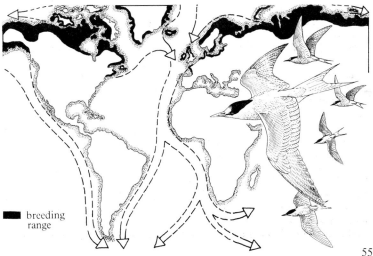

breeding range

55

Major autumnal migration routes of Arctic Tern

The Manx Shearwater is also a great traveller in winter, and ringed birds have been discovered along the South American coast as well as in Australia, but the complete story of its winter movements is still to be discovered. Of course, many seabirds, and particularly the auks and their young, swim quite long distances in the autumn when they leave their breeding quarters.

The Red-backed Shrike is famous for its 'loop' migration. In autumn the Red-backed Shrike of western Europe travels in an easterly or south-easterly direction until it nears the Aegean Sea when it changes to a southerly direction and crosses the eastern Mediterranean. In the return spring passage the shrikes leave Africa some 1000km (600 miles) east of where they entered in autumn, coming up north to the east of Suez and through Syria. There has been much discussion as to why they should undertake this migratory route. Perhaps during the rather formidable desert crossing northwards the shrikes take advantage of the south-westerly winds that predominate at high levels and bring them into the eastern corner of the Mediterranean where the winds over the sea are also favourable.

In some parts of northern Europe where, for instance, the coastline of the Netherlands concentrates masses of Starlings, finches and Lapwings moving out of eastern Europe, one can see some huge numbers of birds passing. During one such movement on the shores of the Issjelmeer in the Netherlands, I saw 56,000 Chaffinches and 26,000 Starlings passing over in a matter of four hours. Only very rarely can you see such a volume of migration in Britain as the largest mass of birds from north-east Europe and Scandinavia generally passes to the south of us along its primary south-westerly direction. However, on the west coast of Wales and in one or two other areas, which concentrate birds, you can see some fairly striking movements. Throughout Britain on October and November mornings, shortly after sunrise, it is possible to see Chaffinches and other birds moving in a south-westerly direction.

The first autumn movement in Britain is, perhaps, less obvious than many others; it usually begins about mid-June, when Lapwings, dispersing from their breeding grounds, fly westwards in small flocks. Travelling at the same time may be Curlew and other marshland waders. This is not a migration in the strict sense but more a dispersal of young birds and unsuccessful breeders.

Most migrants do not stay in one place throughout the winter but perhaps stay for a period of a month or so in one area before passing on to another. Waders may spend several weeks in some estuaries fattening up before moving on to other appropriate habitats further south. For example, British Redwings, Fieldfares and, indeed, visiting Blackbirds and Song Thrushes may stay with us in our local fields for a period before they too move on to other parts, sometimes further south if the weather with us is very hard. A great deal depends upon the availability of food as well as the weather and, as a result, birds will travel by different routes in different years.

Hard weather starts off very large movements to the south-west and south. For example, one January, after heavy snowfalls on the coast of Dyfed, in a matter of fifteen minutes, I counted 2,600 birds, mostly Starlings, Skylarks and Lapwings, flying westwards towards Ireland. Later in the same day I calculated that in one area of about five square kilometres there must have been over a million birds foraging on the fields. From time to time I have seen, even in Cambridgeshire, smaller movements of birds in westerly directions after substantial falls of snow either to the east or north of us.

In recent years, radar has increased our knowledge about migration and made it clear that we, with our binoculars, only see a fraction of a movement. What we may see on the ground has therefore to be interpreted most carefully. Nevertheless, the local birdwatcher should know the primary or standard direction followed by the common visible day migrants, and try to find out what happens to them as they move through the local country and subsequently compare the numbers seen, as well as the directions, with any previous published records. There is still scope for some co-operative efforts amongst members of bird clubs in different parts of Britain to trace what is happening to our local migrants.

In recording the migrations of birds in your notebook, there are a number of things to note. Inevitably, you should record the date, place and time during which the observations took place, as well as the weather conditions, including cloud cover, wind direction and speed according to the Beaufort scale. You can record the flocks as they appear and pass over your observation line. You need to record the species, the number in each flock, direction of flight, height above ground and any calls that they are making. If you have time, try to record comments on any other features that strike you, whether, for instance, the birds continue to fly in the same direction. Is it true, for instance, that Chaffinches, while travelling in their primary direction, tend to head from one wood to the next? It is particularly important if you are near the sea and are watching birds take off over the sea to follow them for as long as you can. Do they change direction after they have gone some distance from land? Do they gain height or go down closer to sea-level? On good days it can happen that the birds are passing in such numbers that you cannot record all the details in full. If you have a miniature tape-recorder you can record your observations and transcribe them later. Failing that you can draw a compass-rose with eight or sixteen points, in your notebook for each species that is passing. To each of the directions you add an arrowhead with the numbers for each flock – it is best to use a new compass-rose every hour or so, or more frequently if required.

Ringing

Although radar has become an extremely useful tool in the study of migration, the marking of a bird with a leg-ring, so that it can be individually recognized, has for a long time been a key method for discovering more about a bird's travels, its life expectancy, its family relationships and so on. The ring is a very light, but strong, band of aluminium or nickel alloy. This band is carefully wrapped around the bird's leg using a special pair of pliers. The ringer makes a note of the ring number, the species of bird and any other facts that he can glean about it, and then sends the most important details to the

British Trust for Ornithology (BTO) which co-ordinates the ringing scheme in Britain. When the bird is found, details of each recovery are sent back to the finder and to the original ringer so that he too can build up a life history.

Ringing is prohibited except under a licence issued by the Nature Conservancy Council through the British Trust for Ornithology. Furthermore, certain methods for trapping birds as well as attempting to trap certain rare birds in their breeding areas requires an additional licence. The BTO publish a very useful account of what ringing has achieved, the BTO Guide No. 16 entitled, *Bird Ringing* by Chris Mead.

In addition to the numbered rings there are other ways in which birds may be marked to make them recognizable as individuals. Some scientists mark the birds they are studying with wing-tags which are usually brightly coloured plastic tags. They are fitted to the forewing in such a way that they lie flat over the wing and do not impede the bird's progress. Numbers written on them, together with the colours of the tag, enable the bird to be individually identified from some distance.

Ringing has shown that young Fulmars leave their ledges when they are about seven weeks old. They spend the next three or four years at sea before they finally return to the cliffs to prospect for nest sites for several seasons. Only then do they begin to breed, in about their seventh year. Their mean expectation of life is about sixteen years, but they have a potential life span of fifty years. Dr David Lack has calculated that the average further life (life after its first year) for an adult songbird is 1–2 years, for various waders and gulls 2–3 years, and for Swifts 4–5 years.

The ringing recovery of a species of which fairly large numbers have been ringed can give interesting information about life expectation, mortality rate, etc. The mortality rate of some birds is very high but is balanced by a high rate of breeding. For instance, if only one young survives from each pair's breeding activity each year the Robin population would increase by more than 50 times every 10 years. The annual mortality rates for another three common species are: 35% for the Blackbird, 53% for the Starling and 44% for the House Sparrow. Two larger species for which figures have been worked out are 15% for the Herring Gull and 6% annual mortality for the breeding population of Fulmars in Scotland.

Some people worry that ringing or the actual wearing of a ring is cruel to birds and that they might be damaged when they are being caught or that the weight of the ring will hinder their feeding. As I indicated earlier, every ringer in Britain has to undergo a strict training programme before he is allowed to ring on his own and while accidents can always happen most ringers now operate with a strong sense of their own responsibility. The rings are very light in weight and should fit fairly snugly; even when I used an aluminium ring and three plastic rings on Wheatears, the total combined weight was, relatively speaking, less than one shoe on a human being or less than the daily variation in a Wheatear's body weight: the Wheatear puts on weight as it feeds during the day and loses it during the night. There really is, generally speaking, no evidence that ringing harms birds.

Territory, song and courtship

Territory

In general, this can be thought of as 'any defended area' in which takes place either mating, nesting or feeding or some combination of these activities.

The use made of territory varies enormously between species. Robins, Wrens, Blackbirds and Wheatears carry out all three activities in their territories, whereas the Goldfinch will leave its territory to search for food. Ruffs and Blackcocks hold territory only to mate, while most seabirds hold territory only to nest.

Several species also defend a territorial area in winter. A notable example is the Robin, but a number of migratory species, including Wheatears and shrikes, also do so in their winter quarters and also in migration.

Finally there is a 'roosting territory'. Starlings return to the same perch to roost at night and defend the spot. Treecreepers return to the same hollow in the soft bark of Redwood trees and attack other Treecreepers which come too close to it.

Not all birds of prey have territories and for most species 'home range' is a better term. Buzzards have territories which they defend but Kestrels do not.

Size of territory

Different species need different sizes of territory but the extent will vary even within species. The territory of male Wrens has been seen to be as small as 0·4 hectare (1 acre) and in other cases to be over 2·8 hectares (7 acres). Golden Eagles may be dispersed 5–6km (3–4 miles) apart and the area which may be available for each pair to range over may be 40–60sq km (15–23sq miles).

The type of habitat, population density and the individual aggressiveness of the owner (these last two factors may be linked) leads to variation in territory size. Indeed, in a way, individual aggressiveness is probably the important factor in the variation in territory size. Although shortage of food within a habitat may occasionally be responsible for a low population, the chief way in which a habitat affects population is its ability to screen the view of one aggressive male from another. For this reason broken ground and thick foliage are important because they reduce the chances of one male seeing another.

Variation of population density in waterbirds such as the Great Crested Grebe is a well known factor affecting territory size. The less successful pairs of some species in terrestrial (rather than aquatic) habitats will move to less suitable ground when the population density is high and there will be a little reduction in territory size. The territories of Robins and many other species are also compressible if population increases and there can also be seasonal changes in area, too. There does not seem to be any direct evidence that territory limits the total breeding population in all habitats. However, where there is clearly a dense population of birds, the chances that a latecomer will be able to carve out a territory are fairly small.

Site attachment

Whilst keeping an area free of intruders is one important characteristic of territory, another is site attachment. A male and female will for part of the year become attached to, and isolated in, one particular part of a habitat which they will often defend. Perhaps for some species territory is important in the formation and maintenance of the bond between the pair.

An attachment to one site is also important in another sense: the owners gain familiarity – particularly if they return year after year – with places where food is available or where shelter can be found. This, for example, increases their 'confidence', to use a very anthropomorphic term; an older Wheatear which had bred successfully in one year was able, when it returned rather late to Skokholm, to dislodge a younger Wheatear, which had already established itself in the territory occupied by the older bird in the previous year.

Some Wheatears live until they are five years old and perhaps longer. In spring they usually return to the same territory and pair with the same mate if it has also returned. However, although Wheatears tend to be faithful to a mate, the evidence really shows that they are more faithful to the territory. At

Thousands of Starlings roost in the centres of cities in Britain where the night temperature is often higher than in woods. Notice how regularly they space themselves; this is their 'individual distance' which the other birds will not invade.

A typical Avocet aggression display involves 'edging', this entails the defending bird walking side by side with the intruder, apparently displaying its black-and-white pattern and occasionally fluttering its wings.

the end of each breeding season they part and disperse independently from the nest area.

Swifts invariably return to a previous nest site and if the previous year's mate returns then the bond is reformed. Several species as different as Bearded Tits and ducks form pairs as many as six months before they actually nest. In spite of this betrothal period they split and go their own ways at the end of the nesting period. Jackdaws may be one of the few species where the evidence suggests that they mate for life.

Defending territory

Some of the more obvious manifestations of territory are song and the various display patterns which birds use to defend their territory. These signs enable us to determine where the boundaries of the territories are, how large they are and what uses pairs make of them. Most male birds advertise their presence by a song which identifies their species, their sex and their sexuality. Also, there is a tendency to attack individuals which intrude in the territory and, if they leave their own territory, a tendency to flee from other birds that attack them.

The song is usually loud and often delivered from a conspicuous perch or during a display flight, such as the 'butterfly flight' of the Greenfinch. Other examples are the song flight of the Skylark, circling over the fields and the tumbling flight of the Whitethroat.

The tendency to attack individuals which intrude is usually manifested by a

Stone-curlews are territorial in the breeding season but in the autumn they gather in flocks before migrating. Here two birds are displaying aggressively with their necks stretched and tails spread.

variety of threat displays; actual fighting only occurs when the threats have failed. Normally the males defend their territories – they sing and proclaim their presence. Generally they are also more brightly coloured than the females and these colours are often used in displays. The males attack both male and female intruders, particularly when the male is unmated. Once, however, a pair occupy a territory, a female will approach another intruding female and see her off. As the female does not usually have the bright colours of the male she does not normally use the same posturing, so their routine is a dominance display followed by a chase; if the intruding female does not retreat, then a fight ensues. The most obvious examples are found in our own gardens: each territory owner seems to try to assert his own dominance over the area first by song and then by display. When an intruder comes into a territory the bird, such as a Robin or Blackbird, hops towards it in a somewhat upright position and at first, patrols alongside it. Often this approach is sufficient to make the intruder flee.

If, however, this display of dominance does not have the desired effect, the owner will start to adopt various extravagant postures: the Robin, for example, lifts its head and neck and displays its red breast, keeping it towards the intruder, whether the latter is perched above or below. The Blackbird adopts various aggressive postures in an upright position with body and neck feathers fluffed out so that the whole body appears larger, also, the tail is usually depressed and slightly fanned. The Wheatear has a somewhat similar upright position and, like the Robin, shows off its pale sandy buff throat and breast, as well as the black and white markings on the head, wings and tail.

Other birds in similar situations also make use of exaggerated postures and emphasize prominent patches and colour. Great Tits, for instance, have what is called the 'head up posture', which reveals more clearly the black throat and belly markings, the sudden revelation of which is often enough to make an attacker hold off in mid-air.

If these displays fail the owner may eventually fly at the intruder and a chase may ensue. Sometimes the intruder leaves the territory but then tries to come back by another route, in this case the chase is prolonged. Finally, if the owner is still determined to hold on to the territory and the intruder remains reluctant to leave a real fight can ensue, with the birds attempting to peck and fly at each other. Very occasionally, these battles result in the death of one or other of the combatants.

During late winter and early spring, many resident birds begin to show signs of establishing their territories and, for the curious ornithologist, there is a large field for observation and interpretation.

Songs and calls

Song can best be defined as a series of notes or sounds consistently repeated according to some specific pattern. It is produced mainly by the male, and usually during the breeding season. Both songs and calls convey messages over longer distances than do the postures that a bird adopts when displaying, although the effect of song is sometimes reinforced by displays. Song is not a language in the sense that we understand it – it cannot convey precise instructions but it can convey a feeling.

Whilst song serves a number of functions, some sexual, some social and some individual, the most important function of all is to proclaim the identity and sex of the singer. It also maintains an emotional relationship between the singer and his mate. Finally, song will identify the individual, itself, to its mate and to its offspring because each bird song differs slightly from that of its neighbour.

For the individual bird, song helps to discharge nervous energy: a bird does manage to perfect song through practice and the possibility that some birds sing for the joy of it should not be arbitrarily ruled out.

Birds have a varied vocabulary of calls; some may be, like song, declarations of territorial rights, and be used when the motivation to defend is low. Calls also indicate needs, other than territorial or sexual; for example, the need for company may be one of the functions of the calls of young birds, which are still dependent on their parents. Alarm calls, especially those indicating certain dangers, such as the near approach of a predator, trigger an immediate reaction which may not only affect birds of the same species but others as well. The 'pinking' of a Blackbird when a Tawny Owl is discovered, gives a particularly obvious example of this type of call. Some of the more extreme alarm calls, which give warnings of predators, apparently also indicate fear and tend to be high-pitched with a relatively narrow frequency range and indefinite endings. This gives them an almost ventriloquial effect, making them extremely difficult to locate.

Anybody who has watched tits feeding in woodland areas will know that it is possible to locate the flock by following the contact notes. These contact notes tell each bird where the others are, and warn them off if they are getting too close. At the same time they attract back to the flock birds which have been wandering off. The utterances of some birds communicate not only the location but also the presence of some other object.

Most of the songs dealt with so far consist of vocal sounds. However, many advertising sounds made by birds are non-vocal. One of the best known examples is the drumming of the Great and Lesser Spotted Woodpeckers. These sounds are made by a very rapid tattoo of blows by the bill on a dead branch usually near its end. The sound can carry 400m (1300ft) or more through a wood. This drumming equates with the advertising song in songbirds. The bill clattering of White Storks, which is a greeting display, when one adult throws back its head in recognition of and greeting to its mate, is often shown in bird films.

The use of the wings to produce sounds are well known to the average birdwatcher. They vary from the wing-clapping of the Woodpigeon to the fast tumbling flight of the Lapwing, whose hard-beating wings are able to produce a 'buzzing' sound on the downstroke. Nightjars and some owls also clap their wings noisily as part of their sexual and territorial displays. The 'drumming' or 'bleating' of the Snipe is perhaps the best example of producing sound from the tail feathers. To produce this the Snipe, while flying over its marshland territory, dives at a gentle angle and fans its tail. The outer pair of feathers are separated from the remaining six pairs and the sound, which lasts about two seconds, is the result of the air rushing past these feathers and causing them to vibrate.

Few birds sing all the year round and most song is correlated to the breeding season, being partly linked with the increasing length of the day. At the turn of the year, many species may resume singing, provided the weather is not too hard. Robins reach their maximum song-output as early as February but most species apparently do not reach it until April or May. The frequency of song falls off when the young hatch. In August, when many birds are moulting, there is little song but later in the autumn singing starts again from Chiffchaffs, Willow Warblers, Wheatears and others and they may even be signs of nesting activities.

It is easy just to enjoy the beauties of bird song and calls, but the birdwatcher may wish to go further and ask a whole range of questions. What are the times and seasons during which birds sing, and from where do they sing? How does the weather affect song? Does the range of song perches change throughout the season and depend on the amount of foliage? Are they exposed when in song, or hidden? How many different types of song does a male have and what are the occasions on which he uses them? Having started to answer these questions, others will follow. The tape-recordist, too, can capture the different varieties of song and calls and, perhaps, build up, by cutting, editing and resplicing, a sound picture of a typical bird from your garden or favourite habitat.

Pair formation

Song tells an unmated female, newly arrived from her winter quarters, of a territory-holding male which is ready for a mate. But when the newly arrived female comes into a territory she is often attacked as if she is an intruding male, and if she is not ready to mate she may well move on. If, on the other hand, the female holds her ground and does not leave the territory or, as in some species, lowers her head, exposing the nape of her neck in a submissive posture, the male will eventually stop attacking her and accept her as a mate. The females of some species, for instance the Chaffinch and the American Song Sparrow, respond with a special call, when they are prepared to accept the attacking male as a mate. The pair then settle down and initially seek out the boundaries of their territory and discover what it contains in the way of food and shelter. Indeed, one gets the impression from watching newly paired Wheatears that they are learning not only about their territory but also about each other.

Once the birds are paired they will usually remain so until the end of the breeding season and then return to their wintering areas independently. Amongst some species which raise two broods, the female will occasionally take a new mate for the second, if the first male has started his moult and has deserted her. Not all birds pair for the season; the male and female Ruff and Blackcock meet at the lek, copulate there and part, and the male takes no further interest in the female, eggs or young, so this must be one of the shortest pairings.

Courtship displays

Whilst song is one way of manifesting sexual feelings, courtship displays are another. In some species they may reinforce the effect of song but in others they are the main method by which the male communicates to the female his need to mate with her.

During these courtship displays the males demonstrate patches of bright colours to their mates by twisting themselves into odd and sometimes fantastic positions. Some of this colour may often remain concealed until the bird takes up this posture. Other patches of colour are only revealed when the tips of the dull autumn feathers, which helped to camouflage the birds during the winter, wear off. Some plumages used in displays are grown every spring between January and April, like the variously coloured necklet feathers of the Ruff. Not only feathers but other parts of the body are used in displays. Puffins grow their large and multi-coloured bills just before they return to their nesting slopes, and some of the herons, and in particular the Little Bittern, can change its bill colour quite quickly when the male encounters the female at the nest.

The courtship displays have a number of important functions. They stimulate sexual readiness, sometimes not only in the bird being courted but also in the bird doing the courting. Often seabirds nesting on cliff-face colonies will not have such a wide range of sexual displays as, for instance, smaller song birds and a number of social displays appear to compensate for

Above Ruffs, so-called because of the necklace of coloured feathers, occupy small territories known as leks. When Reeves, the females, appear at the lek they approach a male and copulation takes place. The females then go off on their own to rear the family.

Left This photograph shows the Robin in a posture commonly seen in spring where, by stretching up its head, it is showing off the full length of its red breast and throat to an intruder.

Right The young of Greenshanks are nidifugous and they leave the nest within hours of hatching but keep together as a family even when they can fly. The young are cryptically coloured.

Below The young of these Buzzards are nidicolous and remain in the nest while the early stages of their growth are completed. Only when food is exceptionally abundant are all the young reared.

this. These large social displays, such as the head-flicking or hiccuping of the Puffins, may also stimulate sexual readiness, not only in their own mates but in other members of the colony. At a seabird colony in the evening you may often see three-quarters of the Puffin colony on a clifftop head-flicking as though they all have hiccups.

Amongst the many displays are those in which the male brings material to the nest, usually with excitement and sometimes with some ceremony. Gulls, terns, gannets, herons and indeed many passerines all bring material and may display it with some excitement to the female.

Most of the true courtship displays bring birds towards the fertilization of the female. After the establishment of the pair they search for nest sites and then build the nest. At intervals they break off to relax, preen and court each other. This may include courtship feeding in which the male brings food and gives it to the female, which, in addition to stimulating and strengthening the pair bond, may be helpful to the female at a time when the eggs are forming within her body. The male also becomes accustomed during this period to bringing food to the female so that when the eggs are laid he can feed her on the nest without hesitation. The male normally approaches the female with food in a rather upright posture, showing excitement by flicking his wings. The female in return crouches and stretches out her wings and quivers them. She is now rather below the male, and holds her beak skywards to receive the food. This is an attitude of solicitation which is common, with variations, to many bird species. The male then feeds her and she relaxes.

The next stage in this sequence of events is copulation. In the case of the female Goldfinch she solicits with her legs bent, wings out of the coverts and quivering, head up, beak open, calling a high-pitched 'tee-tee-tee-tee'. The male approaches her excitedly as usual, but instead of feeding her he mounts her and they copulate. This is a rather general picture of the way that courtship displays lead up to copulation and there are a number of variations between species. Some experts think that courtship feeding, acts as a release for coition, and it occurs just prior to it in a number of species.

Several species of birds have displays, in which the bills are touched, which lead to courtship feeding and copulation. The billing of the Puffin where a pair or up to six or so individuals may knock their bills together or where Gannets spar with their bills are examples of this.

Courtship displays may also involve certain types of flight. Many land and water birds use a 'moth' flight in which the bird flies comparatively short distances with wings quivering rapidly, but not very deeply. This flight is often used, if not always, in circumstances which have some sexual connotation, for instance often just before, or just after, copulation. There are variations too on this flight: for instance, the Wheatear flies fast and erratically over his territory in what I call the 'zig-zag' flight.

The 'butterfly' flight or 'bat' flight, in which the wings beat deeply and more slowly, is more often used in territorial circumstances. The Greenfinch uses it regularly in spring. Besides finches it is used by the auks as they fly onto their cliffs. Hen Harriers and many other species have similar display flights.

Nesting behaviour

Nests

Any nest must be able to protect the eggs and young from both the rigours of the climate and predators. A nest may be just a cup-shaped depression scraped in the soil or a highly intricate structure woven together with a variety of different materials. Almost any position that affords protection and support can hold a nest, from holes in the ground to flimsy branches at the tops of trees. Most nests that are built above ground are found in suitable forks in trees and bushes. The larger nests are found on the thicker branches while some nests, like the Redpoll's, are found 12m (40ft) up

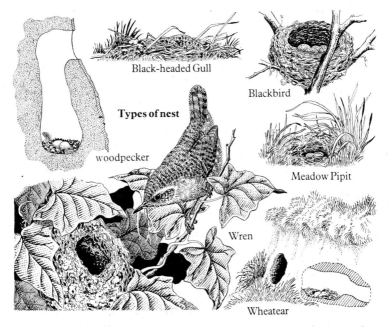

Black-headed Gull

Blackbird

Types of nest

woodpecker

Meadow Pipit

Wren

Wheatear

Eggs in ground nests tend to be cryptically coloured, giving them added protection. Eggs in hole nests tend to be brightly coloured which may help the adults to locate them.

The Red-backed Shrike's range has contracted markedly in Britain and western Europe over the last hundred years, possibly linked with the cooler and wetter summers.

The full extent of the Manx Shearwater's winter wanderings in the southern oceans is still unknown; to discover the direction in which its home burrow lies the Shearwater practises a simple form of navigation using the position of the sun as a guide.

Bird observatories such as that at Portland Bill are established to study migration by ringing and recording weights, etc. of birds which have been caught in Heligoland traps and mist nets. Most bird observatories welcome voluntary help.

at the ends of branches, where they sway about violently in strong winds. Somes nests are open – like those of the Woodpigeon and the Turtle Dove; others are domed like those of the Magpie, Long-tailed Tit and Wren. Holes in trees are also regularly used, woodpeckers and Willow Tits bore their own, but many other species including Starlings, tits and owls use old holes that have either rotted away or been excavated. Treecreepers quite often nest under bark which is peeling off.

Those birds which nest on rocks surfaces or in burrows use hardly any nesting material. Puffins and Manx Shearwaters are able to dig their own burrows in some loose types of soil. The Wheatear makes use of a variety of holes in the ground as well as in walls. Its preference, however, is for a burrow with a comparatively small entrance and an escape chamber behind the nest, into which the incubating female or mobile young can run if a predator comes down the burrow. Some ground-nesting birds may, by swivelling themselves around on their breast, make a scrape in the ground, to which they bring

The Greenfinch builds a fragile nest about 2½m (8ft) above the ground. They are often found in Hawthorn bushes which are popular nesting and feeding habitats for many small birds.

Wheatears nest in holes in the ground but will use a variety of artificial sites such as dry-stone walls, drain-pipes and even tins. The holes sometimes have an escape chamber behind the nest in case predators enter the burrow.

material. Waders such as Lapwings and Avocets, if they are close to their nest scrapes, may pick up pieces and lay or toss them on the nest. Avocets seem to be able to build quite substantial nests in this way. Some material probably helps to camouflage the nest and eggs, such as when Stone-curlews and Oystercatchers line their nests with a few chips of rock which may be supplemented by a collection of rabbit pellets.

Kingfishers and Sand Martins excavate holes in sand banks close to water where they obtain their food supply. Along the sea-cliffs, especially where there are horizontal bedding planes, can be found colonies of seabirds. These bedding planes provide numerous ledges on which the auks and other species such as the Kittiwake nest. Because of the precariousness of the situation the young of these birds have developed special behaviour patterns to stop them from falling off.

Establishing a nest site

Some birds return to the same nest site in succeeding years, particularly if they are on fairly permanent structures. Oystercatchers will return to the same tree or cliff ledge. Swallows return to the same mud cup. Some of the returning birds would appear to be the same individuals that have used the site in previous years but, on the other hand, some sites would appear to be

Above Knot and one Sanderling foraging in wet sands. Length and size of bill and length of legs help to prevent direct competition between them and other shorebirds foraging in the same area.

Right Greenfinches in a Cambridgeshire wood tended to eat the hips of the Field Rose *Rosa arvensis* but left the hips of the Dog Rose *Rosa canina*. Have you noted any other food preferences?

'traditional', in that they have been used by succeeding generations of birds. Indeed, the Loch Garten Osprey site has been used for twenty years by a number of different individuals, although this would appear to be a special case as it is a protected site.

A traditional nest site – one which is used on several occasions over a number of years by different pairs – presumably must have certain characteristics which suit the requirements of the species making it an 'ideal' nest site, or it may be that it is the only suitable site in the area. With larger birds, the choice of suitable nest sites is more limited and therefore it is advantageous for a pair to use an already established site. In a large tree which changes shape or form slowly there is time for some small bird nest sites also to become 'traditional'. It only remains for the observer to know and record the nest sites of an area well enough and long enough for them to be recognizable in the future.

Building a nest

Mud is a well-used building material. Blackbirds and Song Thrushes line their nests with it, while Nuthatches plaster the entrance of their nest holes with it to reduce the size. The Swallow and House Martin are well known for using mud pellets to make up the cup of their nests which are often found under the eaves of houses.

Most song birds make use of what material there is to hand. For instance, as well as using grasses, Goldfinches also use Forget-me-nots and Sweet Alyssum, which they place corolla outwards on the nest. This has the effect of camouflaging the nest amongst the leaves of fruit trees, limes and cherries. Goldfinches also make use of spiders' webs to bind the first pieces of nest material to the twigs of the tree.

The actual construction of the nest is an instinctive action; birds of the same species build nests that conform closely to a given pattern without any instruction. However, there is some evidence that birds build better nests as they grow older and more experienced. The movements which they use to build the nest, therefore, tend to be rather stereotyped. There appears to be three movements which are common to most passerines: 'pulling and weaving', 'scrabbling' and 'turning'. In 'pulling and weaving', loose strands of nest material are pulled towards the breast of the bird, which is sitting in the cup of the nest, and then pushed down into the cup. The female 'scrabbles' by pressing down into the cup and pushing back hard with each leg alternately. In 'turning' the female turns round while sitting in the cup and thus shapes the cup of the nest. The female normally builds the nest, sometimes helped by the male. In a few species the male does the major part of the building assisted by the female. The notable exceptions, perhaps, are the unlined nests built by male Wrens and some other species which are used by the males for roosting. The time taken to build a nest may range from virtually a day or so to perhaps several months, or even years, in the case of a bird of prey which may add an odd stick to an already existing nest throughout the breeding season. Small passerines which winter in Britain may take as long as a month if bad weather intervenes and stops building. Summer visitors to this country, because they arrive later, build their nests rather more rapidly. Generally speaking, the further north the species is nesting, the quicker the nest is built because the breeding season is shorter. In cases of necessity, when for instance a nest or clutch of eggs has been destroyed, repeat nesting and even second clutch nests can be built swiftly.

Eggs and egg-laying

Very few birds nest all the year round. Most have a restricted breeding season, which in Britain and the temperate world is in spring and summer. Breeding is so timed that the young are usually raised when their food is most plentiful. Various external factors which differ with latitude and with the environment control the breeding season. In our temperature zone increasing warmth in spring is apparently one of the factors which brings the birds into breeding condition. For example, resident species like the Song Thrush and Blackbird, breed earlier in mild early springs than in cold late ones.

The essential parts of an egg are the yolk, albumen and shell with a membraneous lining. Just before the eggs leave the oviduct the colour which is provided by two basic pigments – a blue or blue green and a brown olive – is deposited on the shell. Spots are produced by the pigment gland while the egg is stationary in the oviduct, but if the egg is moving streaks are produced. The function of the colouring is chiefly to camouflage the eggs and many which are laid in the open, such as those of the Little Tern and Ringed Plover which are generally stone or dun-coloured with spots, are extremely difficult to see. Many others, such as the Lapwing, Partridge, Skylark and Meadow Pipit, have a buff-brown basic colour. Birds of prey produce a series of warm red-brown eggs which, unfortunately, prove very attractive to egg collectors. Those eggs which are well hidden in holes or in deep nests and do not need camouflage are often pale or even white, and it is thought that these light-coloured eggs might help the parent find them more easily in the dark hole.

Incubation period

Normally small birds will lay one egg each day, often in the early morning. Large birds may lay theirs every other day as the larger eggs take longer to form.

Large birds with long incubation periods, characteristically lay one clutch a year: others may lay two, three or infrequently more clutches, and probably all but a few species of birds will replace the first if it is destroyed shortly after it is laid.

The number of days needed to incubate the eggs may be as few as eleven in some of the warblers, but up to fifty-three days, in the case of a Fulmar incubating a single egg. Normally the species which have open nests incubate their eggs for the shortest period: Wrens and Long-tailed Tits, for instance, which have domed and soundly constructed nests, may have incubation periods lasting fourteen to eighteen days. Full incubation usually begins, in

Above Modern farming tends towards hedgeless prairies; the gardens of villages have the aspect of a woodland edge or the early stages of the development of a wood and provide a refuge for many species of wildlife.

Below When the Suffolk marshes were flooded during the last war, many, like Minsmere, proved attractive to birds. In 1948 the RSPB leased Minsmere and thoughtful management has provided still more habitats. The RSPB purchased Minsmere in 1977 from part of their £1 million appeal.

While the European Kingfisher nests in burrows near streams, other species are terrestrial, feeding on insects, and it is probable that our Kingfisher's large bill was originally evolved as an adaptation to insect-catching and not for fishing.

passerines, just before the last egg is laid, which helps to ensure that the eggs hatch at about the same time.

The male's duties in this early part of the nesting period are to defend the territory and the nest. At this point, the males, some of which have been silent since pair formation, start singing again. At times they give the appearance of considerable idleness. Now song has not only the effect of keeping intruders out but also, at least in the early stages of the incubation period, of giving the female confidence in her new situation.

Young and their development
During the incubation period the egg gradually becomes lighter and the shell weaker. A day or so before hatching the embryo develops two structures which help it to break out of the shell: firstly, a strong muscle at the back of the neck, and secondly, a blunt, horny, calcareous spike – the egg-tooth – on the tip of the upper bill; both disappear within a few days of hatching.

The first external evidence of hatching is a star-shaped crack that appears on the side of the egg near the larger end which is caused by the embryo's egg-tooth pressing against the inside of the egg-shell. The beak moves very slowly and very spasmodically around the inside of the egg and gradually the top is cut off. Just before it breaks out the embryo's first calls establish contact with its parents. Depending upon the species, and the weather, hatching may take from as little as an hour or two to two or three days; grebes hatch out within a few hours.

Once hatched, nestlings of different species show different degrees and methods of development: one group known as 'altricial' young are helpless when hatched. They are also called 'nidicolous' in that they remain in the nest for an extended period. They are entirely dependent on their parents for food and have a brightly-coloured gape surrounded by a soft and puffy light-coloured edge which shows the adults where to put the food. They are usually naked at hatching or have only a sparse down on the dorsal regions which may possibly help to keep them warm and also hide them.

On the other hand, 'precocial' young are capable of walking or swimming soon after hatching. They may be dependent on their parents for food for a day or so or may immediately join the parents in searching for food. These young birds are also called 'nidifugous' in that they leave the nest almost immediately after hatching. They are covered with a dense down which is cryptically coloured, and, when the parent calls the alarm notes, they 'freeze' and become extremely difficult to see.

Altricial young
The majority of altricial species can fly at about seventeen days and become actually independent of their parents at about twenty-eight days. Nestlings hatched in a hole undergo a longer period of nest life than a chick hatched in an open nest and, as a general rule, the larger the species the longer it takes to develop. The Cuckoo is one notable exception, its young develop very rapidly because some development of the embryo may start while the egg is within

the female. As a result the egg, which is laid later than its hosts', often hatches out first.

The young of small perching birds pass through five stages of development. During the first three or four days the nestlings grow rapidly, their feather quills are visible beneath the skin and gradually force their way through. Their chief instinctive activities are stretching up their heads and neck and gaping when a parent brings food and, second, stretching out to defecate. They might also make their first food calls. In the second stage their eyes open and their weight increases rapidly. They begin to preen the opening feather quills, and the control of body temperature is established.

In the third stage, more motor co-ordinations appear: the nestlings cower in fear; they can stretch their wings upwards and sideways; they can scratch their heads, shake themselves, fan their wings and flutter them when begging. A new series of call notes also appears. They are now capable of regulating their body temperature, and are well-feathered individuals. Some may be independent of the nest and their nest mates and be able to care for their feathers and move about to escape enemies. They can inform their parents of their whereabouts and respond to the parents' alarm notes. At this stage they will leave the nest if disturbed prematurely.

During the fourth stage, the nestlings that still remain leave the nest. At first, behaviour is characterized by silence, except when calling for food, and by general immobility. Their chief advance is the acquisition of flight. They also begin to show various independent feeding activities such as wiping the bill, pecking at objects, and picking up food.

The fifth and final stage of their development begins with the attainment of flight. They may still pursue the parents for food and this is the chief time when the young are conditioned by parental behaviour as to what they should fear and can be frequently heard calling in fear. They also develop antagonistic attitudes, such as threat postures and fighting. Finally they become independent of their parents.

Precocial young

The newly-hatched precocial chicks, such as Lapwings, Moorhens and so on, by contrast with the development of nidicolous or altricial young birds, are rather well-proportioned except for the wings which are relatively small and undeveloped. The chicks are thickly covered with down feathers on all the feather tracts. The chicks show quick response to visual and auditory stimuli, the eyes are open and both vision and hearing are already developed. The body temperature is partly established but the birds still need brooding for a few days.

Most precocial chicks remain in the nest from about three to twenty-four hours after they have hatched, while they dry off. They rapidly become increasingly active, standing up and walking and running about. If they are waterbirds they may even swim. They peck at objects in the first stages of learning in order to discover what they can eat. Feeding begins on the first day out of the nest, and quite surprisingly, they search for, find and pick up food independently of their parents. They can already respond to the food-calls of parents and take food from the parents' bills or from the ground where the parents have placed it. During the first three days after hatching the young birds begin to display virtually all the activities associated with the parents, except for breeding and flying. They sun themselves, swim, use feet for scratching themselves. They can call alarm notes, 'freeze' and peck at each other. Harmless fighting occurs and a definite social bond is evident. In many of these birds the brood persists as a unit until autumn or winter comes along.

What really has happened is that with precocial birds the first three stages of development of the altricial birds have already passed in the egg.

Parental care

In the nidicolous species one of the first duties of parents is to dispose of the egg shells which could otherwise give away the position of the nest; they are either eaten or carried away as soon as they have been vacated by the nestlings. The nidifugous young vacate the empty eggs and the nest itself fairly rapidly so there is little point in moving the empty egg shells, though many do.

After the eggs have hatched the males sing less often and show less aggressiveness in the defence of the territory, although they become more aggressive towards predators and human beings as the time approaches for the young to leave the nest. Even though they take only a small part in incubation, the males share in the feeding of the young and obviously they then have less time to sing or to fight with territory competitors. In the first few days after hatching the female broods tight, particularly until the young gain temperature control. In open nests, even after brooding proper has finished, the females will shelter the young from the sun and rain, spreading their wings in order to do so.

Parents do not feed nidicolous young immediately after hatching. Normally they bring the first food after an interval of two or three hours: in some species the interval may be much longer. But once they start bringing food the parents work at an increasing rate until by the time the young are ready to leave the nest they are rushing from one food source to the next in a frenzied fashion. The young birds soon become aware of their parents' approach and they instinctively respond by a begging behaviour which initially involves the thrusting up of their necks with open mouths which show their bright-coloured gapes and tongue spots and which in their turn provide targets at which the parents can aim the food.

In birds of prey the incubation of their two or three eggs which are laid two days apart usually begins with the first egg laid and consequently, if three eggs are laid, the first-hatched gets a lot more food than the last-hatched bird. Once started, this disparity in size is maintained throughout the period that the youngsters are in the nest. Thus, if there is an abundance of food the female eagle may be able to rear all three nestlings, but if there is a shortage then perhaps only the first-hatched will survive, having eaten its nest siblings.

Nest sanitation is important in order to prevent disease, and to lessen the chance of the nest being discovered. In nidicolous young, defecation usually occurs immediately after feeding although it may not occur after every food particle is brought. Generally speaking, the faecal sac, depending on age, is a mass of semi-solid uric acid and darkish intestinal excreta enveloped in thick mucus which is easily portable by parents. These sacs are regularly disposed of by the parents either throughout the nest life or, in some species, only in the first part of the nestling period. When the nestlings of some species are very small the parents will eat the excreta.

There is no necessity for nidifugous species to produce faecal sacs. Seabirds void their excrement over the edge of a cliff ledge and other nidifugous birds are constantly on the move and there is little chance of an accumulation of faeces.

Break-up of the family

The time when the young leave the nest and become independent of their parents is the period when they are in greatest danger. For almost all species, the mortality rate between leaving the nest and sexual maturity is very high. Three-quarters of the young birds of prey, for instance, die before they reach sexual maturity.

Some young birds which nest on the ground are able to walk or stagger some distance away from the nest. Birds which have been reared in nests in trees or on cliffs flutter down, while others fall down hard and are still able to survive. Young auks, in particular, seem to be well padded with a layer of fat so that if, in their glide and flutter down from ledges to the sea, there is an error and they hit the rocks below, they often seem to bounce off alive with no broken bones. Swifts can fly from the moment they leave the nest and are, from that moment, independent. They have, however, stayed in the nest for a fairly long incubation period of five to eight weeks. Some seabirds, especially petrels and shearwaters, are deserted by their parents some days before the young leave the nest burrow so that they too have to hunt for food by instinct alone.

For the most part young when they leave the nest do not travel far at first. But they disperse ever more widely, learning to find their own food until, finally, they become independent of their parents.

With Blackbirds it would seem that there is some attachment among the family and that this may persist for some weeks after the young have left the nest. Young Yellow Wagtails may keep together until the onset of the moult. Robins leave the nest when they are fourteen days old and finally become independent when they are about five weeks old – although the female may well have deserted them when they are about three-weeks old in order to raise another brood.

Some wader families, like that of the Greenshank, for instance, which do not have second broods, travel together from one area to another in search of food until the young become proficient in hunting and can look after themselves. The bigger birds of prey often remain in the area of the 'home range' for several weeks before they disperse.

What birds eat

Discovering what birds eat really tests your desire to be a birdwatcher-naturalist. The subject, though fascinating, can be extremely complicated and requires enormous patience. However, this should not put you off. There are some comparatively simple things to do. Identifying what plants or animals a bird may be eating may not be too difficult, but the researcher will also want to have an accurate idea about the quantity of each item.

Size and appetite
Whilst every living creature needs food to keep it alive, a small bird which burns up energy at a furious rate needs to take about a third of its body weight in food every day to make up for the heat and energy loss. The exact amount depends on the type of food eaten. Large birds need less food because their heat loss is less; being larger creatures they have less surface area in relation to their volume than small birds. At certain times of the year and for certain activities they need to take in extra food. Some need to accumulate extra fat before they migrate and fly long distances; while some males feed their mates before they lay their eggs. Young Manx Shearwaters and similar species put on an enormous amount of fat before they are deserted by their parents and have to learn to fend for themselves.

Habitats
Birds have managed to exploit almost every habitat and every niche as a hunting ground; they have not been able to dig more than a little way into the ground in search of food, but at sea Long-tailed Ducks regularly dive to 20m (66ft) and can reach 60m (200ft), but information of the depth at which other diving birds feed is rather limited. Perhaps here is an opportunity for scuba-diving birdwatchers to collect knowledge. Birds hunt in the sky as high as there are insects and other creatures in a sufficient quantity to make it worth their while. To be able to exploit all these niches birds have developed within a general form a huge variety of beak shapes, legs and wing structures. Adaptation to different food sources has probably affected their structure more than any other factor, even the urgent need to escape from predators.

Anatomy
The structure of the body, particularly its effect on the way the bird moves, may restrict it to a certain type of habitat; the structure of the beak and talons

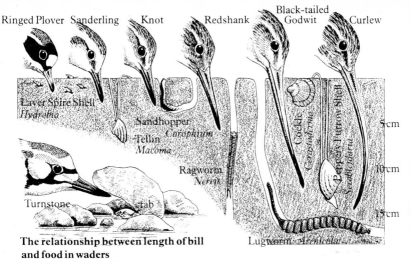

Ringed Plover · Sanderling · Knot · Redshank · Black-tailed Godwit · Curlew

Laver Spire Shell *Hydrobia*

Sandhopper *Corophium*

Tellin *Macoma*

Ragworm *Nereis*

Turnstone · Crab

Cockle *Cerastoderma*

Peppery Furrow Shell *Scrobicularia*

Curlew

5 cm

10 cm

15 cm

Lugworm *Arenicola*

The relationship between length of bill and food in waders

Waders have different bill sizes and lengths of leg, which enable them to forage in different places on the shore line.

restrict it even more and finally local experience of the availability and whereabouts of food items is also very important. This local knowledge of the food supply is often not taken into account when people who have been caring for sick or injured birds release them into the wild after several weeks or several months of treatment. This particularly applies to recently cleaned seabirds. We tend to think that the shoals of fish on which the auks feed are everywhere. But they move with the seasons. Auks come into the waters near the breeding cliffs when the sand eels and other small fish are near the surface and most abundant, and from daily contact they get to know in which part of the colony's home waters the fish are to be found. Once a seabird is removed from the sea for any great length of time it will lose touch with the fishing flocks and be considerably handicapped in finding sufficient food when released.

The way in which the beaks, legs or wings have been adapted now most affect the selection of food. Herons and egrets have long legs that enable them to wade deeply into lakes, ponds and even the sea to hunt. Wading birds with their long legs, such as the Bar-tailed Godwit, can also wade deeply in water and still probe beneath the surface and into the mud or sand with their long sensitive bills. Another wader, the Avocet sweeps the surface of the mud below water from side to side with its awl-shaped bill.

At the other extreme Goldfinches, Redpolls and their relatives have rather short legs. They tend to perch on rather thin and flexible twigs which bend over so that the bird has to hang on to the twig with its short toes, often nearly upside down. Their short legs help to keep the centre of gravity rather low so that there is less strain on the legs. Short-legged birds also use their feet more commonly in holding food than long-legged birds. Incidentally, the Goldfinch has a rather thin and pointed bill which enables it to probe quite well for the seeds of some of the compositae – dandelions and thistles.

Long pointed wings are the mark of fast 'pursuit' birds, while the broad-winged birds are either those which soar in the rising thermals or which live in woodland areas and need the ability to manoeuvre through branches. Included in the first group are long-winged insect-eaters such as Swifts, Swallows and Nightjars which need some speed to pursue their prey which they catch with their mouths in mid-air. Included in this group are also the falcons which use their talons to catch birds, insects, and rodents.

The evenly balanced arrangement of claws are important in woodpeckers, as it enables them to get a better grip on the bark of trees on which most of them hunt. Their strong bills are also useful when digging holes beneath the bark for insects or their larvae, or hammering at acorns which they wedge in cracks in branches or trunks. Green Woodpeckers have largely deserted the trees and prefer ant nests on the ground into which they insert their long tongue and, with its sticky tip, extract the ants or their pupae.

Waterfowl, particularly those which swim and dive for their food, have developed webs between their toes: some species may only be partially webbed like the Red-necked Phalarope which is essentially a wader which feeds in the water. At the other extreme, the Shag which hardly ever walks any distance on land has webs between all four toes to drive it through the water when it is hunting for fish amongst the sea wrack. Razorbills and Guillemots propel themselves through the water in their search for fish by beating their wings almost as though they were flying. While the Dipper, which hunts for its food amongst the stones in swift-flowing streams, holds out its wings in such a way that the flow of water forces it to the bottom.

Investigating birds
The range of different feeding methods and the different food taken is extremely varied and a study of them supports the view that closely related species living in the same habitat do not compete for food. Following this point through there is enormous scope for working even in your own garden or some other habitat well-known to you which is utilized by birds for hunting. What, for instance, are the commonest ways of finding food used by the different species? What sort of hunting perches do the Spotted Flycatchers use? What height are the hunting perches? Do they hunt in the trees or just use part of the tree as a look-out? Do the hunting perches change through the breeding season and does a change indicate a different type of prey? When answering the same sort of questions for other species you may have to list the plants birds use and attempt to determine their use as food or hunting perches throughout the season. Does it change? Do birds hunt in the same place or with the same regularity throughout the day?

It is sometimes impossible to do all this in a professional way in which you can completely document the food species of birds but gradually you will build up a picture of the distribution of birds throughout the habitat.

Birds in your garden

Many readers will live in fairly modern houses with new gardens comprising flower beds, a small vegetable plot, with a lawn and perhaps a pond or bird bath. Probably, this patch will be duplicated many times in the neighbourhood. Overall, it is similar to one or more stages of a woodland edge with rock outcrops (the houses) or a stage in the growth of a woodland. Many gardens have trees of varying ages and heights – the older the better. Some gardens may have shrubs up to 6m (20ft) high. Some will have a field layer up to 1½m (5ft) and some may have a heavily mown (or grazed) lawn. This is the same sort of structure that you find in woodland, particularly at the edge of natural woodlands which may be spreading into a grassland habitat.

Trees

I believe that if you are really trying to provide a garden for birds you must aim towards this basic concept of a woodland edge. You may not have enough room for big trees and may have to concentrate on the lower levels. Perhaps your neighbours are providing trees in their gardens. However, if you do have a tree and it grows too big you can always cut it down and use some of the wood for firewood and leave the rest to provide homes for insects. Then plant another tree. Creating a bird garden takes a long time and if you have come into a fairly new garden and have to plant it yourself you are going to have to wait for several years for it to achieve maturity. However, you have to start somewhere and the garden you lay down may set the pattern for your successors.

When choosing trees for your garden try to plant native ones. It is on native trees, with their associated invertebrate fauna, that most of our birds are accustomed to feed. An Oak takes a very long time to grow but even in its earliest years it is a very beautiful tree and is also a host to a very large number of insects. What native trees you can grow depend upon the soil and climate of your region. The Nature Conservancy Council have produced a useful booklet, *Tree Planting and Wildlife Conservation*. Walnut trees, too, provide delicious nuts providing that you can beat the squirrels and Rooks to them. As in forestry they can be planted fairly close together to start with and thinned out after a few years so that they grow good lateral branches which make foraging much easier for the less agile of the woodland birds. Trees will provide not only an extensive feeding ground but many species will also find in them the height they need to display their dominance.

The first trees to be considered are the fruit trees which in time develop lateral branches with plenty of cracks in which insects can hide. What I am saying is heresy to the keen fruit gardener who all too often tends to shoot birds in fruit trees. But at least two scientists have recently shown that tits, and Blue Tits in particular, eat large numbers of Codling Moth *Cydia pomonella* caterpillars and as apples are damaged more by Codling Moths than by birds I have erected nest boxes for them on my apple trees. Pears as well as other fruit trees can also use the help that birds will give them by eating insects. However, they will not control insects – no predator controls the number of its prey – it may, however, help to dampen the numbers down a little.

Shrubs

Hawthorn *Crataegus monogyna* is a most valuable shrub to have in the garden. It can be allowed to grow to its full height as a shrub providing a mass of beautiful colour in spring and luscious berries for the Blackbird and Song Thrush, as well as the Redwing and Fieldfare during the autumn. It can also be layered into a hedge where, if it is trimmed once or twice a year (not too early in the year), it will provide thick cover for quite a range of birds such as Blackbirds, Robins, Dunnocks, Wrens, Linnets, Greenfinches, Chaffinches and Whitethroats. If it is allowed to grow more than 2m (7ft) high it can also attract the Lesser Whitethroat – in the south-east part of the country, at least. It is also important to allow it a good thick bottom growth.

Another useful natural shrub is the Elder *Sambucus nigra* with its beautiful cymes of white flowers which, if you do not pick them to make Elder-flower wine or Elder-flower pancakes, will turn into sweet tasting berries which are much favoured by both birds and winemakers. Also when large, the Elder branches and twigs become a hunting ground for warblers and are also suitable as nesting sites for birds such as the Goldfinch.

Ivy *Hedera helix* has a gloomy reputation, perhaps because it is rather dark and is often found on ruins. Nevertheless it does provide a nesting site for many species and the Song Thrush and Blackbird eat its berries quite voraciously in late March and April, perhaps because there is little else to eat at that time of the year. However, if it is allowed to completely cover the bole of the tree it will eliminate a feeding ground for woodpeckers, Treecreepers and Nuthatches.

Brambles *Rubus fruticosus* in some senses are an awful pest but they do produce nest sites and Blackbirds and other thrushes do eat their berries. Rowan *Sorbus aucuparia* is another shrub, more properly found in the mountainous districts of the north or higher ground, which bears colourful berries eaten by birds. The Sea Buckthorn *Hippophae rhamnoides* is found on the sandy shores of the east coast and masses of migrants feed on it as soon as they make a landfall on their autumn migration. One native tree under-rated for its berry is the Whitebeam *Sorbus aria*. It is an attractive tree with white flowers and red berries which seem to be voraciously eaten by birds.

A range of berry-bearing shrubs, which generally do not grow more than

2m (7ft) high, including the genera *Berberis* and *Cotoneaster* are important. *Berberis vulgaris* and *Darwinii* both produce berries which are taken by birds but not all the species are equally palatable. The same applies to *Cotoneaster*.

Our knowledge about which birds take which species of berries is still surprisingly open and someone who would really like to watch these bushes throughout the year could add greatly to the subject. However, you must pay attention to what happens to berries at the end of the winter too, when birds may be so hungry that they eat the less palatable ones.

Plants

The third structural level is the field layer with plants up to 2m (7ft) or so. I personally am not so likely to wish to plant native species in my garden, although I allow some to flower and produce seed. Queen Anne's Lace or Cow Parsley *Anthriscus sylvestris* is one of the most beautiful and stately plants of the English countryside and I was glad to see Greenfinches which nest in my thick hawthorn hedge eating its seed. I keep a rough area alongside part of my hawthorn hedge and this I cut only once a year. Cow Parsley grows here and in various other rough spots.

Another plant which real gardeners absolutely hate is Fat Hen *Chenopodium album*, but finches are immensely attracted by its seeds and, if you can bear to have it around, it will bring in Greenfinches, Linnets and Goldfinches in late summer and early autumn. Bullfinches like Black Bryony *Tamus communis* which, although it is a most attractive creeper, is generally disliked by gardeners. Native Teazel *Dipsacus pullonum* attracts Goldfinches which will also eat some of the more exotic varieties. Many species of the Compositae family are sought after by finches, particularly the Sunflower *Helianthus annuus*, aster *Aster* spp. and many species of thistle, although not many gardeners will tolerate Creeping Thistle *Cirsium arvense*.

The bottom or 'open' layer of the garden will usually be lawn or soil. Both are good for birds hunting for insects and other arthropods, as well as for seeds.

Ponds

Ponds provide water for drinking and bathing. Most birds obtain sufficient moisture from their food but some such as Woodpigeons and Turtle Doves come down regularly to drink, and many others will drink water if it is available. Many people try to attract birds by letting water drip into a container. To do this all you need is a bucket or a container which can hold a fair amount of water. You can set up a syphon and control the rate of dripping with a length of plastic tubing and a small tap, which can be obtained from any home-brewing shop. It is best to let the water drip into a shallow receptacle such as the edge of your pond or even an upturned dustbin lid, sunk into the ground. This is very attractive to warblers and finches.

In my pond I have put stones which just appear above the surface which allows birds to bathe. Tony Soper recommends a flower pot upside down in the water with a stick or twig through the hole on which Wrens and other

Simple pond with dripping water

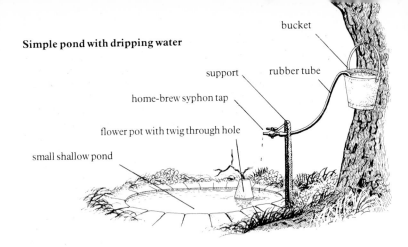

A system for providing dripping water which will attract birds especially in dry weather can be made simply from 'home brew' equipment.

small birds such as warblers can perch and slither down to drink.

It is surprising what species will come to your pond particularly when it has matured and the water plants are growing well, encouraging insects of various kinds. On my small pool I found a Green Sandpiper one morning in the last half of June. If you have fish or tadpoles in your pond you may expect visits from Kingfishers and Herons. Both have visited my pond. I have never detected the Kingfisher as causing any serious damage. If he caught anything which my family or I were particularly interested in we certainly did not detect it. The Heron can, however, clean out a Goldfish pond in no time at all. As he is really adapted for eating eels and we like our Goldfish, we try to prevent him from eating them. You can cover the pond with wire netting, but this is unsightly. It is said that a strand of nylon line – fishing line will do – set 60cm (24in) back from the edge of the pond and stretched tightly 15cm (6in) above the ground, will stop the Heron. This is because Herons tend to alight away from the water and after looking around move towards it. If their feet hit something fairly invisible and firm they take fright and move off. Never leave loose nylon line lying about as this can 'tie up' birds' legs and cause serious damage. Herons are protected by law so don't shoot them. Another will come along in due course, therefore it is much wiser, in the long run, to protect the pond.

Bird tables

I have been writing about using nature to make your garden attractive to birds, and also making nature provide the food and shelter. You can also attract birds by setting up bird tables and nest boxes. Bird tables can be made easily or can be purchased from the RSPB. They are essentially a board with an edge to prevent the food being knocked off. Some have shelters over them which prevents the food becoming wet. They should be set at least 1m (40in) above the ground to make it more difficult for cats and squirrels to get at them. The wooden support can be sheathed in a length of slippery plastic drain pipe. The problem of Starlings and House Sparrows taking too much food is difficult to overcome. I have no satisfactory solution although some people have made wooden tops to their bird tables with holes big enough for Blue Tits to get through but then only Blue Tits can feed, and hanging food baskets really cater for them. I have tried putting food out in different places which disperses the different species for a time. It is essential to clean and sterilize bird tables from time to time to avoid the risk of *Salmonella* infection. You should not leave out so much food that it is left lying about.

A variety of different makes of seeds are available from pet shops and are advertised in the different bird magazines, and I imagine that most people will, if they are going to buy seed, buy it in bulk from a supplier. I used to make up my own mixture at one time, with Black Rape, Millet, Hemp, Niger, Sunflower and Peanut.

On the bird table you can put not only seeds, but household scraps and

Nest boxes can be made from a variety of simple plans which are specifically designed for a range of birds.

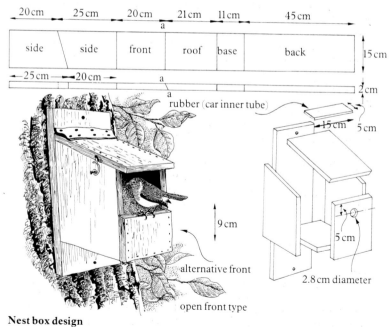

Nest box design

fruit, whether berries or the rotten part of apples. Do leave rotten apples under the trees – thrushes, particularly the winter visitors, love them.

Some people hang out nuts – for some reason those in red bags prove very attractive to Siskins – and others jam nuts or fat into the bark of trees in their garden. This is fine for tits and others that can hang on to the sides of the tree, but Blackbirds and other thrushes need flat surfaces.

Nest boxes
Putting up nest boxes is a good idea particularly in new gardens which have not developed a wide range of nest sites. Most people buy the standard tit nest box, not realizing the other possibilities. Different species of bird need different designs of nest box. One simple type of nest 'box' can be made from half a coconut, with a hole in the base for drainage. If it is placed in a wall climbing shrub like a wisteria it will make an ideal nest site for Spotted Flycatchers, which often make use of old Blackbirds' nests. They also use small open-fronted nest boxes with base dimensions of 15 × 9cm (6 × 4in). Swifts use nest boxes if they are provided. These should be 46 × 20cm (18 × 8in) wide by 15cm (6in) deep with an entrance hole in the base and an inspection lid at the opposite end. It should be fitted under the eaves of the house at least 3m (10ft) above the ground. Artificial House Martin nests are more difficult to make unless you have a kiln in which you can bake clay. However, they are occasionally advertised for sale. The Tawny Owl is another species whose breeding distribution you can help by making a nest box. This should be made from wooden planks at least 75cm (30in) long and 20cm (8in) wide with a square base which must have at least half a dozen drainage holes. The box should be lined with peat or sawdust before it is hung in position under a bough at about 30° from the vertical. The details of these and other nest box designs can be found in the BTO Field Guide No. 3 *Nestboxes*.

Vegetation
Comparatively few people would appear to have attempted to thicken artificially vegetation around trees, or thicken forks in branches in hedges by inserting handfuls of dried leaves for Wrens. This is more common on the continent. By tying a spruce branch to a trunk with strings about 30cm (12in) apart it is possible to provide a space in which thrushes might nest. There are many other ways in which these simple aids to nest building can be applied.

Dangers
Perhaps, at this point I ought to say something about two problems that arise in bird gardens. The first one is the problem of pesticides. There has been a lot of concern over the last twenty years about the effects of certain organo-chlorine chemicals. Many of them are now banned, at least for garden use. However, all pesticides should be used with discretion and it is best to use them only when you really need to against a pest which you are sure is harming your plants. It is a waste of money using insecticides on something

which is doing no damage. Do not use a pesticide unless you know what it is; the active ingredient should be stated on the container label. There are some pesticides which the RSPB feels are relatively non-poisonous to birds and mammals and are not persistent. These are Derris or Rotenone, Pyrethium, Malathion and Carbanyl. The RSPB produce a leaflet called *Pesticides and the Gardener*.

The second problem concerns the activities of cats. One extreme view says that cats should be got rid of at any cost. The other extreme says that cats only kill birds if they are not fed properly, which in my experience is nonsense; good feeding will probably make the cat a more effective hunter. There is no proof one way or the other as to what effect cats have on local bird populations. When I have to take action to save a nest I rely on 'shushing'; occasionally a lump of dried earth lobbed to fall just short of the cat so that the lump breaks open and harmlessly spatters the offender with dust will do the trick – if the throwing motion has not been enough to frighten it away. Cats, like birds, can be a nuisance in the wrong place. But there is no justification for using cruel methods to get rid of them.

There are a number of very good books which take bird gardening much further, for example, *Gardening with Wildlife* by the RSPB, the *RSPB Book of Garden Birds* by Linda Bennett published by Hamlyn, Tony Soper's *The New Bird Table Book* published by Pan, and David Glue's *Garden Bird Book*, published by Macmillans.

Books to read

Field guides
Bruun, B. and Singer, A. (1970, revised 1978), *The Country Life Guide to the Birds of Britain and Europe*, Newnes
Ferguson-Lees, J., Willis, I. and Sharrock, J. T. R. (1983), *The Shell Guide to the Birds of Britain and Ireland*, Michael Joseph
Hayman, P. (1979), *The Mitchell Beazley Birdwatchers' Pocket Guide*, Mitchell Beazley and RSPB
Heinzel, H., Fitter, R. and Parslow, J. (1972), *The Birds of Britain and Europe with North Africa and the Middle East*, Collins
Peterson, R., Mountford, G. and Hollom, P. A. D. (1954, 4th edition 1983), *A Field Guide to the Birds of Britain and Europe*, Collins

Other books
Brown, L. (1976), *British Birds of Prey*, Collins
Campbell, B. and Ferguson-Lees, J. (1972), *A Guide to Birds' Nests*, Constable
Cramp, S., Bourne, W. R. P. and Saunders, D. (1974), *The Seabirds of Britain and Ireland*, Collins
Cramp, S. and Simmons, K. E. L. (1977), *Handbook of the Birds of Europe, the Middle East and North Africa*, O.U.P.
Fisher, J. and Flegg, J. (1974), *Watching Birds*, T. & A. D. Poyser
Fuller, R. J. (1982), *Bird Habitats in Britain*, T. & A. D. Poyser
Glue, D. (1982), *The Garden Bird Book*, Macmillan
Gooders, J. (1967), *Where to Watch Birds*, André Deutsch
Grant, P. J. (1982), *Gulls: A Guide to Identification*, T. & A. D. Poyser
Harrison, C. J. O. (1975), *A Field Guide to the Nests, Eggs and Nestlings of British and European Birds*, Collins
Harrison, P. (1983), *Seabirds: An Identification Guide*, Croom Helm
Hickling, R. (1983), *Enjoying Ornithology*, T. & A. D. Poyser
Hollom, P. A. D. (1952, 4th edition revised 1968), *The Popular Handbook of British Birds*, Witherby
Mead, C. (1983), *Bird Migration*, Newnes
Pemberton, V. (Annual), *Bird Watcher's Yearbook*, Buckingham Press
Perrins, C. (1974), *Birds*, Collins Countryside Series
Porter, R. F., Willis, I., Christensen, S. and Nielsen, B. P. (1974), *Flight Identification of European Raptors*, T. & A. D. Poyser
Prater, A. J. (1981), *Estuary Birds of Britain and Ireland*, T. & A. D. Poyser
RSPB (1983), *RSPB Nature Reserves*, RSPB
Sharrock, J. T. R. (1977), *The Atlas of Breeding Birds in Britain and Ireland*, British Trust for Ornithology, Irish Wildbird Conservancy and T. & A. D. Poyser
Sims, E. (1983), *A Natural History of British Birds*, Dent
Thompson, Sir A. Landsborough (1964), *A New Dictionary of Birds*, Nelson
Wallace, I. (1982), *Watching Birds*, Usborne (For the younger birdwatcher)
Warham, J. (1983), *The Techniques of Bird Photography*, Butterworths

National bird magazines
Bird Life. Published bi-monthly by the Young Ornithologists' Club.
Bird Study. Published quarterly by the BTO.
Birds. Published quarterly by the RSPB.
British Birds. Published monthly from Fountains, Park Lane, Blynham, Bedford MK44 3NJ.
Irish Birds. Published by the Irish Wildbird Conservancy.
Nature in Wales. Published by the National Museum of Wales.
Scottish Birds. Published quarterly by the Scottish Ornithologists' Club.

How to use this guide

The arrangement of birds in the following sections is that given in *A Species List of British and Irish Birds* (BTO Guide 13) (1971). This is the sequence most widely used in Great Britain and Ireland since the adoption in 1952 of the *Check List of the Birds of Great Britain and Ireland*. Commencing with the divers it progresses through the orders until the Passeriformes, the largest order and most advanced birds of all, are reached, concluding with the Tree Sparrow. (There are two exceptions; for the convenience of arranging the plates, the Fulmar is placed with the auks on pages 152 and 153, and for ease of comparison of the females the Pintail and Shoveler have been placed with the Mallard and the Gadwall on pages 104 and 105.)

It was not intended that each of the 480 or so species now admitted to the British list should be dealt with in this book. Only those regularly seen in these islands, and which a birdwatcher who is reasonably mobile can expect to see in the course of a season or two's work without much difficulty, are included. These may be loosely fitted into five categories, indicated by the coloured borders to the pages, which are as follows: **ducks, geese and swans** (green); **birds of prey and owls** (red); **seabirds** (dark blue); **water birds including herons, rails and waders** (light blue); and **land birds, including some non-passerines** (brown).

Each of the species described is illustrated in colour on the opposite page, and where necessary in flight, the latter as a black and white illustration. Such flight pictures are especially important for difficult groups of birds like waders and wildfowl. In some species, such as the ducks, the male and female are very different. In these cases, both have been illustrated and denoted by the symbol ♂ for the male and ♀ for the female.

The description of each species has perforce needed to be brief, the total amount of information given depending on the number described on each page. Thus, only the major features are mentioned, mostly under the general headings of flight, voice, habitat and distribution.

Divers family Gaviidae

Black-throated Diver *Gavia arctica* 56–68cm (22–27in) Like the other two divers, a large, almost wholly aquatic bird with a bulky body and stout neck. In summer with boldly patterned upperparts, grey head and back of neck, with the front of the neck and throat black edged by black and white streaks. In winter the upperparts are dark. Special note should be made of the bill which is more slender than that of the Great Northern, while the forehead is less steep. **Flight** Takes off with difficulty from water but once airborne flight is strong and rapid with the head held lower than the body, giving an unmistakable 'humped' appearance which is also typical of the other two species. White underparts contrast with dark upperparts; no wing-bar. **Voice** A guttural 'kwuk-kwuk-kwuk'. **Habitat** Lakes in summer; winters mainly on the coast though not infrequently inland on large lakes and reservoirs. **Distribution** Breeds locally in Scotland north from Argyll and Perth but not in Orkney or Shetland. Winters mainly off Scotland and the east and south-east coasts of England; rather rare elsewhere.

Great Northern Diver *Gavia immer* 68–81cm (27–32in) In summer has a black head with incomplete white neck bands and spotted underparts. In winter much like the Black-throated but generally larger size and much heavier bill are distinguishing features. **Flight** and **Voice** As for Black-throated. **Habitat** Lakes in summer; winters mainly on the coast, occasionally at inland waters. **Distribution** Mainly a winter visitor to Scotland, Ireland and south-west England. Birds occasionally summer in northern Scotland, a pair nesting in 1970.

Red-throated Diver *Gavia stellata* 53–58cm (21–23in) Our smallest diver; in summer has uniform dark grey upperparts, a grey head and sides of neck. The dull red throat patch may look black when viewed from a distance or in poor light. The back of the head and neck are streaked black and white. In winter looks whiter than the other divers and has a finely spotted back. At all seasons the up-tilted appearance of the rather slender bill is an important identification feature. **Flight** As for Black-throated. **Voice** A quacking 'kwuk-kwuk-kwuk'. **Habitat** Small pools to larger lakes on moorland; winters offshore though frequently visits inland waters. **Distribution** A few pairs breed in County Donegal, otherwise the highlands of Scotland including many islands are its stronghold. In winter may be found off all coasts, particularly in sheltered bays, harbours and larger estuaries.

winter

Black-throated Diver

summer

winter

summer

Great Northern Diver

winter

winter

Red-throated Diver

summer

Grebes family Podicipitidae

Great Crested Grebe *Podiceps cristatus* 48cm (19in) Breeding adults have pronounced double-horned crests and reddish facial frills, the former reduced, the latter lost completely in winter. The thin red bill, very white cheeks and neck distinguish it from the slightly smaller Red-necked. **Flight** Conspicuous white wing-patches, while the long neck and trailing feet are typical of all grebes. **Voice** A barking 'gorr' and a crooning song. **Habitat** Large areas of open water required for breeding; in winter some move to sheltered coasts. **Distribution** Resident in many counties south from central Scotland; winters on all coasts.

Red-necked Grebe *Podiceps grisegena* 43cm (17in) Stockier built than Great Crested from which it may be distinguished in winter by the darker colour of the head extending below the eye, the sides of the neck dusky not white, and a black-tipped yellow bill. **Flight** Similar to Great Crested. **Voice** A high-pitched 'keck-keck'. **Habitat** In winter off coast; rare inland. **Distribution** Winter visitor, mainly to the east coast.

Slavonian Grebe *Podiceps auritus* 33cm (13in) Chestnut neck and underparts, black head with golden ear-tufts; bright colours lost in winter when it may be distinguished from Black-necked by its conspicuous white cheeks and straight bill. **Flight** Shows a white patch on trailing edge of wing. **Voice** A low rippling trill. **Habitat** Lakes and ponds in summer; mainly maritime in winter. **Distribution** Breeds on a few lakes in north-east Scotland; winters off all coasts.

Black-necked Grebe *Podiceps nigricollis* 30cm (12in) Black head and neck with downward pointing ear-tufts. The slightly up-tilted bill, steep forehead and black cheeks distinguish it in winter from Slavonian. **Flight** Longer wing-patch than Slavonian; wing-tips very dark. **Voice** A soft 'peeip'. **Habitat** Shallow lakes in summer; mainly on coast in winter. **Distribution** Breeds only at several sites in central Scotland; sporadic elsewhere; winters mainly on east and south coasts.

Little Grebe *Tachybaptus ruficollis* 27cm (10½in) Stockier built than the larger grebes. Dark brown with a chestnut throat and whitish yellow patch at the base of bill in summer; paler in winter. **Flight** No wing-patch. **Voice** A rippling trill. **Habitat** A wide variety of lowland waters; some move to harbours and estuaries in winter. **Distribution** Breeds in most areas.

Great Crested Grebe

winter

summer

Great Crested Grebe
summer

summer
Red-necked Grebe

winter

winter

winter

summer
Slavonian Grebe

Black-necked Grebe
summer

winter

summer
Little Grebe

Manx Shearwater *Puffinus puffinus* (family Procellariidae) 35cm (14in) Nocturnal at its colonies, spending the day in its nesting burrows or fishing out at sea. **Flight** A slender-bodied bird with long wings; at times tilting so that dark upperside then white underside is visible. Rapid flight; a few wing-beats followed by a period of gliding, often low over the waves. **Voice** Screaming, gurgling and crowing noises, chiefly heard at colonies. **Habitat** Pelagic, breeding on remote islands. **Distribution** Breeds on a small number of islands off western Great Britain and Ireland. Moves in winter to the east coast of Brazil.

Gannet *Sula bassana* (family Sulidae) 90cm (36in) Adults have gleaming white plumage with narrow black-tipped wings. The head and neck are yellowish buff. Immatures in their first year are dark blackish brown; adult plumage is attained in the fourth year. (The juvenile opposite is not to scale.) **Flight** Strong, the long wings and cigar-shaped body being distinctive. Feeds by plunge diving from heights up to 42 metres (140 feet). **Voice** A loud 'urrah-rah-rah-rah-rah', normally only heard at the colonies. **Habitat** Marine, rarely coming inland. Breeds mostly on small remote islands. **Distribution** Sixteen colonies in British Isles. Majority nests in Scotland. First year birds are migratory, moving to north-west African waters; most older birds in winter disperse generally through Britain and Biscayan waters.

Cormorant *Phalacrocorax carbo* (family Phalacrocoracidae) 90cm (36in) Slender-bodied bird having dark brown-black plumage with a white face-patch, and in the breeding season a white patch on the thighs. Immatures are pale brown above and white beneath. Swims rather low in the water and when at rest on land frequently adopts a drying posture with outspread wings. Dives from the surface with a distinct forward leap, in contrast to divers and grebes which disappear almost imperceptibly. **Flight** Fairly swift with rapid wing-beats. **Voice** A loud 'urrah', mainly at the nest. **Habitat** Offshore; also estuaries, harbours and frequently inland on rivers, lakes and reservoirs. **Distribution** Resident with colonies scattered along all coasts except between south-east Yorkshire and the Isle of Wight.

Shag *Phalacrocorax aristotelis* 76cm (30in) Dark glossy green, which looks black at a distance, with yellow at the base of the bill. Has a distinctive crest early in the breeding season. Immatures brown, only slightly paler beneath. **Flight** Similar to Cormorant but faster wing-beats. **Voice** A harsh croaking and various hissing noises at the nest. **Habitat** Off rocky coasts with rather few occurrences inland. **Distribution** Resident, breeding on all rocky coasts; usually as a scattering of pairs rather than large colonies, and with few between Northumberland and the Isle of Wight.

Manx Shearwater

juvenile

adult

Gannet

Cormorant

Shag

Herons family Ardeidae

Grey Heron *Ardea cinerea* 90cm (36in) A grey back and wings. Underparts, head and neck white. Black band runs from the eye to end in a trailing crest. On the ground its long neck and legs are distinctive. Its prey—fish, small mammals, amphibians and reptiles—may be sought by wading through marshy ground, or by standing motionless in shallow water. **Flight** The neck is retracted while the legs trail; the large rounded wings, with outer parts black, are moved majestically giving an impression of tremendous power. **Voice** A harsh 'krarnk'. Croaking notes are delivered at nest. **Habitat** Found almost anywhere there is water of some form, be it mountain tarn or estuary. **Distribution** Resident breeding in trees throughout much of Great Britain and Ireland. Where there are no trees it will choose low sites amongst scrub or even nest on sea-cliff ledges. Britain's largest colony with 178 pairs is at RSPB reserve Northward Hill in Kent.

Bittern *Botaurus stellaris* 76cm (30in) A large golden brown bird with much darker mottles and bars. Very skulking in its habits. Normally adopts a rather hunched posture but when alarmed will stand erect with its bill pointed skywards. **Flight** Neck retracted, legs trailing in typical heron fashion. Broad brown wings move with a slow owl-like beat. **Voice** A harsh 'aarrk'; the much remarked upon booming is performed by the male only during the early spring and may be heard over great distances, depending on conditions. **Habitat** Requires large areas of dense reedbed with occasional pools of shallow open water. **Distribution** Formerly restricted to Norfolk and Suffolk, these counties still remaining the stronghold, but since the 1940s has bred in several others north to Lancashire and more recently to Wales. Breeds on RSPB reserves at Minsmere, Suffolk and Leighton Moss, Lancashire. In winter, particularly during hard weather, birds disperse widely from the breeding areas and may occur in quite small marshy patches.

Spoonbill *Platalea leucorodia* (family Threskiornithidae) 86cm (34in) White colouring and long broad bill, spoon shaped at the tip, are easy identification characters. Adults have a yellowish breast-band and in the breeding season head plumes; immatures lack these and have blackish wing-tips. **Flight** Neck outstretched in contrast to the herons; flies rather slowly with regular wing-beats. **Voice** Silent. **Habitat** Reedy areas, lagoons and estuaries. **Distribution** Non-breeding but regular visitor to East Anglia where it may occur in small parties; less frequent elsewhere.

Grey Heron

Grey Heron

Bittern

Bittern

Spoonbill

Ducks, geese and swans family Anatidae

Mallard *Anas platyrhynchos* 58 cm (25 in) The largest, commonest and best known duck. Male readily recognizable by its green head and white ring around the neck. Female brown with distinctive blue speculum. During 'eclipse' or autumn moult the male looks similar to the female but has a yellow bill; female's is greenish and juvenile's reddish. **Flight** Rapid. The blue speculum bordered with white is found in both sexes. **Voice** Female a loud 'quack'; male a subdued 'queek'. **Habitat** Breeds close to inland waters of all sizes; moves to more open waters and to estuaries in winter. **Distribution** Resident in all areas.

Gadwall *Anas strepera* 51 cm (20 in) Male is dullest of dabbling ducks with grey plumage contrasting with black tail coverts. Female smaller than Mallard and with white underparts and black and white speculum. **Flight** Similar to Wigeon (page 44). **Voice** Female a soft 'quack'; male a deep nasal 'nheck'. **Habitat** Ponds and lakes with good cover. **Distribution** Breeds mainly in East Anglia; otherwise a winter visitor in small numbers to most parts.

Pintail *Anas acuta* 66 cm (26 in) A tall slender bird, males have an elongated tail and dark brown head. Females are pale brown with slender appearance, thin neck and pointed tail. **Flight** Fast. Male has green, white bordered speculum: female brown speculum. **Voice** Mainly silent. **Habitat** Chiefly fresh water in summer; larger lakes and estuaries in winter. **Distribution** A few breed in Scotland and eastern England; otherwise a winter visitor.

Shoveler *Anas clypeata* 51 cm (20 in) The enormous bill is the outstanding feature of both sexes. Both are heavier-looking than other dabbling ducks. Drake has green head, white breast and chestnut underparts. **Flight** Rather laboured, the wings having a setback appearance. Both sexes have blue forewings and green speculum. **Voice** Female similar to Mallard; male a gutteral 'took-took'. **Habitat** Shallow water with good cover. **Distribution** Breeds in small numbers throughout much of Great Britain and Ireland.

Mallard

♂ ♀

Gadwall

♂ ♀

Pintail

♂ ♀

Shoveler

♂ ♀

Teal *Anas crecca* 35cm (14in) Our smallest duck, males at a distance seeming to have a dark head in contrast to their grey body. Female similar to small Mallard. **Flight** Very agile, often in compact flocks. Both sexes have green speculum. They appear shorter necked than other species. **Voice** Female a high-pitched 'quack'; male a musical 'kritt'. **Habitat** Breeds amongst thick vegetation; winters on inland waters and estuaries. **Distribution** Resident; rather scattered in south; numerous in winter.

Garganey *Anas querquedula* 38cm (15in) More slender than Teal and in this country never in large flocks. The male's conspicuous eye-stripe distinguishes it from other species. **Voice** Female similar to Teal; male a low crackling. **Flight** Rapid and agile. Both sexes have blue-grey forewings and green specula. **Habitat** Shallow pools, ditches and creeks having plenty of cover. **Distribution** Summer visitor with less than 100 pairs breeding in south-east England; elsewhere a scarce passage visitor.

Wigeon *Anas penelope* 46cm (18in) Compact duck with a short bill. Male's buff cream and chestnut head and grey underparts distinctive. **Flight** Long narrow wings have a conspicuous white patch and green specula. **Voice** Female a purring note; males a distinctive whistling. **Habitat** Breeds close to inland waters; in winter largely estuarine and often seen grazing on fields. **Distribution** Breeds chiefly in northern Scotland; otherwise a numerous winter visitor, particularly large numbers on the RSPB's Ouse Washes reserve, Cambridgeshire.

Scaup *Aythya marila* 48cm (19in) Rather similar to Tufted Duck. Good identification characters are the grey back of the male and white facial mark of the female which is more pronounced than that of Tufted Duck. **Flight** In compact but irregular flocks or lines. Male distinguishable in good light from Tufted Duck by grey back. **Voice** Female a harsh 'karr-karr'; male generally silent. **Habitat** Breeds beside lochs and rivers; winters mainly on sheltered coasts. **Distribution** Occasionally breeds in Scotland; otherwise a winter visitor; up to 25,000 in the Forth.

Tufted Duck *Aythya fuligula* 43cm (17in) Only duck adorned with a tuft at back of head. **Flight** Rapid and like most diving duck has to patter along the water surface before taking off. **Voice** Female a growling 'kur-r-r-'; male in spring has a gentle whistle. **Habitat** Breeds on secluded lakes; winters on open fresh water. **Distribution** Breeds in eastern Britain; winters in all areas.

Teal

Garganey

Wigeon

Scaup

Tufted Duck

Pochard *Aythya ferina* 46cm (18in) The striking plumaged males are among the most easily identified diving ducks. The only duck with chestnut head, black breast and grey underparts. Female larger and paler than Tufted with no white facial markings. **Flight** Straight with rapid wing beats. **Voice** Generally silent; female in spring has a harsh 'kur-r-r'. **Habitat** Breeds in dense vegetation close to fresh water; occasionally coastal lagoons. **Distribution** Breeds mainly in south-east England; winters in all areas.

Goldeneye *Bucephala clangula* 46cm (18in) Has a distinctive head profile, the short bill and steep crown giving an almost triangular appearance. Neck distinctively white. **Flight** Wings produce a characteristic whistling sound. **Voice** Generally silent. **Habitat** Breeds in woodland close to water; winters mainly in estuaries and offshore. Seen on lochs in Scotland in spring and has bred in Inverness-shire woodland close to water. **Distribution** Winters in all areas.

Common Scoter *Melanitta nigra* 48cm (19in) The male, generally greatly outnumbering the browner female, is our only completely dark duck. **Flight** Strong, usually in lines low over the sea. **Voice** Female a harsh growl; male a variety of cooing notes. **Habitat** Breeds on lochs in hilly country; otherwise frequents the open sea close inshore. **Distribution** Small numbers breed in north-west Ireland and Scotland; non-breeders summer elsewhere; winters off all coasts.

Long-tailed Duck *Clangula hyemalis* 53cm (21 in) Only duck combining a white body and dark wings and having an extremely short bill. Male has an extremely long tail. In winter it appears largely white, but in summer plumage it has a dark head and breast. **Flight** Usually low and swinging from side to side. **Voice** Female a soft 'quack'; male a musical 'ow-ow-ow'. **Habitat** Mainly maritime. **Distribution** Winter visitor mainly to east coast; smaller numbers in west.

Pochard ♀ ♂

Goldeneye ♀ ♂

Common Scoter ♀ ♂

Long-tailed Duck ♀ winter ♂ winter ♂ summer

Eider *Somateria mollissima* 58cm (23in) Has a characteristic head profile, the bill continuing in a straight line from the forehead, and a thick set body. **Flight** Usually in single file just above the sea. **Voice** Female a grating 'kr-r-r'; male a moaning 'coo-roo-uh'. **Habitat** Maritime, rarely inland. **Distribution** Breeds in the northern counties of England and Ireland and throughout Scotland; non-breeders summer further south where wintering birds are also regularly encountered.

Red-breasted Merganser *Mergus serrator* 58cm (23in) Long slender profile and slender hooked bill separate it immediately from all other duck except larger Goosander. **Flight** Slender shape and large white wing-patches. **Voice** Female a harsh 'kar-r-r'; male usually silent. **Habitat** Breeds in vicinity of fresh water; frequents estuaries and seacoasts in winter. **Distribution** Breeds mainly in north-west Scotland and Ireland, but extending south in some western areas. Widespread elsewhere in winter.

Goosander *Mergus merganser* 66cm (26in) Larger than Mallard with a similar shape to Red-breasted Merganser, the head and neck patterns separating it from this species. **Flight** Usually low and showing a good deal of white. **Voice** As for Red-breasted Merganser. **Habitat** Lakes and rivers in wooded areas for breeding; mainly open fresh water in winter; not on coast in any numbers. **Distribution** Breeds throughout much of Scotland; has recently extended into northern England and Wales. Winters in many areas.

Smew *Mergus albellus* 41cm (16in) Shorter billed and more typically duck-shaped than other mergansers. White appearance of male should present no identification problems. Females—'redheads'—may possibly be confused with grebes but have a pure white throat and cheeks. **Flight** Takes wing very readily and has a rapid flight. **Voice** Silent. **Habitat** Lakes and reservoirs in winter. **Distribution** Winter visitor mainly to south-east England; rather scarce elsewhere and irregular in the west.

Shelduck *Tadorna tadorna* 61cm (24in) A large, strikingly marked duck, with an upright 'goose' posture. Females are a little duller than males and lack the knob at the base of the beak. **Flight** Slower wing-beats than other duck. **Voice** A loud 'ak-ak-ak-ak'. **Habitat** Estuaries, sandy and muddy coasts, though may travel several miles inland to breed. **Distribution** Breeds throughout Great Britain and Ireland in suitable areas. Is absent or occurs only in small numbers during late summer when the majority makes a moult migration to Germany, with some going to Bridgwater Bay, Somerset.

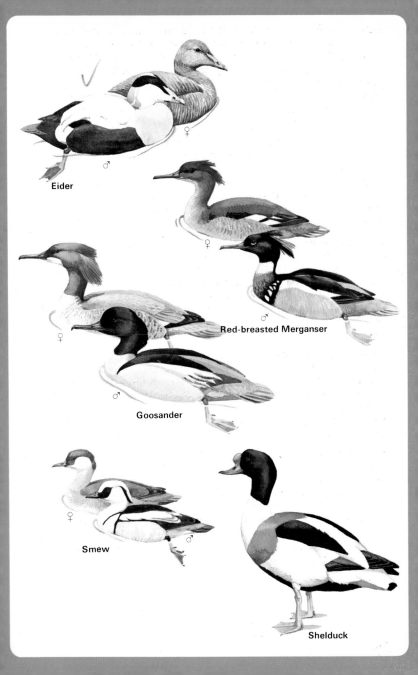

Eider

Red-breasted Merganser

Goosander

Smew

Shelduck

Greylag Goose *Anser anser* 76–89cm (30–35in) Largest of the grey geese having a heavy head and thick bill. Difficult to tell from other grey geese when viewed from a distance. **Flight** Pale grey forewing noticeable when a good view obtained. Often in flocks which adopt a 'V' formation. **Voice** Rather similar to the domestic goose, a loud 'aahung-ung-ung'. **Habitat** In breeding season, moorland areas with numerous small lochs. and in some cases small islands at sea. In winter, marshes and wet meadows from which it regularly flights to agricultural land. **Distribution** Breeds mainly in north-west Scotland where the outer Hebrides are its stronghold. Introduced birds have recently become established in several other parts of Britain. Main wintering area is in central Scotland.

White-fronted Goose *Anser albifrons* 66–76cm (26–30in) Darker coloured than Greylag and Pink-footed, adults having conspicuous black bars on the belly and a white patch at the base of the bill, though both features are absent in immatures. **Flight** Generally more active than other geese and although occurring in large flocks often disperses into family parties. **Voice** A laughing, rather high-pitched 'kow-kow'. **Habitat** Marshes, water meadows and saltings. **Distribution** The Greenland race winters mainly in Ireland and west Scotland, the European race in southern England and Wales.

Bean Goose *Anser fabalis* 71–89cm (28–35in) Browner and darker than other grey geese, with a somewhat long and slender build. Bill is longer and stouter than in Pink-footed. **Voice** Usually a gruff 'ung-unk', though not as noisy as most other geese. **Habitat** Marshes and wet meadows. **Distribution** Rather scarce winter visitor, occurring regularly only in south-west Scotland, Northumberland and East Anglia.

Pink-footed Goose *Anser brachyrhynchus* 61–76cm (24–30in) Rather like small Bean Goose, indeed some authorities consider them races of the same species. Main colour difference is the pale blue-grey upperparts contrasting with the dark head and neck. **Flight** The blue-grey forewings are conspicuous, though should not be confused with those of larger Greylag. **Voice** Perhaps the most noisy of all 'grey' geese, having a varied vocabulary including a musical 'wink-wink-wink'. **Habitat** Similar to Greylag, though is particularly fond of stubble and potato fields. **Distribution** Winter visitor, the first arriving in September, with particularly large concentrations in central Scotland, in Lincolnshire and East Anglia.

Greylag Goose

White-fronted Goose

Bean Goose

Pink-footed Goose

Brent Goose *Branta bernicla* 56–61 cm (22–24 in) Our smallest goose and, apart from the whitish neck patch, the only one to have its whole head and neck black. **Flight** Rather duck-like, usually in irregular flocks. **Voice** A croaking 'rronk'. **Habitat** Tidal flats and estuaries; rare inland. **Distribution** Winter visitor mainly on the east and south coast between Northumberland and Devon; scarce elsewhere.

Barnacle Goose *Branta leucopsis* 58–69 cm (23–27 in) Easily identified, even at a distance, by its contrasting black and white plumage. Has a particularly short bill. **Flight** Similar to other geese, though generally more reluctant to take off. **Voice** A barking 'ark' rapidly repeated. **Habitat** Pastures and marshes close to the shore. **Distribution** Winter visitor mainly to western Scotland and Ireland; scarce elsewhere but like other wildfowl some birds may be escapes or free-flying birds from collections.

Canada Goose *Branta canadensis* 92–102 cm (36–40 in) Much larger than the other two 'black' geese and has a mainly brown, not black and white, body. **Flight** Regularly flies in 'V' formation. **Voice** A trumpeting 'ker-honk'. **Habitat** Grassland close to freshwater lakes and pools. **Distribution** Breeds throughout much of England and parts of Wales; rather few in Scotland and Ireland. Mainly sedentary, though birds from Yorkshire visit the Moray Firth.

Mute Swan *Cygnus olor* 152 cm (60 in) Differs from the other two swans by having an orange bill with basal knob, while the carriage of the neck is less upright. **Flight** Heavy with 'sighing' sound produced by the wings. **Voice** Normally silent. **Habitat** A variety of inland waters, also sea lochs, estuaries and sheltered bays. **Distribution** Breeds throughout Great Britain and Ireland.

Whooper Swan *Cygnus cygnus* 152 cm (60 in) Usually holds neck stiffly erect. The bill, in contrast to that of Mute, is black with a large area of yellow at the base. **Flight** Wings create a swishing sound. **Voice** Our noisiest swan; has a bugle like 'ahng' in flight. **Habitat** Sheltered coasts, inland waters including the larger rivers. **Distribution** Small numbers summer in northern Scotland and has bred on several occasions; otherwise a winter visitor, mainly to Scotland and northern England.

Bewick's Swan *Cygnus bewickii* 122 cm (48 in) Resembles small Whooper, but the smaller area of yellow on the bill ends bluntly above the nostrils. **Flight** Similar to Whooper. **Voice** A rather goose-like gabble. **Habitat** Open waters and floodlands. **Distribution** Winter visitor mainly to England; scarce in Scotland.

Brent Goose

Barnacle Goose

Canada Goose

Bewick's Swan

Whooper Swan

Mute Swan

Ducks and geese in flight. (All are to the same scale.)

Mallard ♂

Gadwall ♂

Pintail ♂

Common Scoter ♂

Goldeneye ♂

Shoveler ♂

Pochard ♂

Goldeneye ♀

Shoveler ♀

Long-tailed Duck ♂

Wigeon ♂

Teal ♂

Garganey ♂

Scaup ♂

Tufted Duck ♂

Eider ♂

Red-breasted Merganser ♂

Goosander ♂

Smew ♀

Smew ♂

Red-breasted Merganser ♀

Goosander ♀

Shelduck

Greylag Goose

Bean Goose

Barnacle Goose

Pink-footed Goose

Brent Goose

Eagles and their allies family Accipitridae

Golden Eagle *Aquila chrysaetos* 75–88cm (30–35in) Adults varying shades of brown, yellowish on the nape. Immatures have a white tail terminating in a black band, and white patches on the wings. **Flight** Powerful, gliding or soaring with occasional, leisurely wing-beats. When soaring, wings held horizontally in a shallow 'V'. Large size, projecting head, longer tail and uniform colouring distinguish it from Buzzard. **Habitat** Mountainous regions and remote coastal areas. **Distribution** Mainly in Scottish Highlands and western Isles; a few pairs in south-west Scotland and at least one pair in northern England where specially protected by RSPB wardening. Rare away from breeding areas.

Buzzard *Buteo buteo* 51–56cm (20–22in) Rather variable in plumage, particularly the amount of white on the underparts. **Flight** Often in soaring leisurely sweeps when the broad rounded wings, short head and broad, slightly rounded tail are characteristic. Often has a dark carpal mark. **Voice** A characteristic 'mewing' note. **Habitat** From barren hills and coastal districts to lower well-wooded areas. **Distribution** Breeds throughout much of Scotland, north-west England, Wales and the south-western counties of England east to Gloucestershire and Sussex. In Ireland breeds only in Ulster.

Sparrowhawk *Accipiter nisus* 28–38cm (11–15in) Adults have closely barred underparts; immatures are rather like the female but more boldly marked below. **Flight** Differs from falcons by having broad rounded wings. Normal flight a few wing-beats then a long glide. Hunts by flying fast, usually low amongst woodland or along hedgerows, dashing through openings or over bushes. Quite frequently soars and may rise to a considerable height. **Habitat** Usually in well-wooded cultivated country. **Distribution** Mainly in Scotland, western England, Wales and Ireland; has decreased and is now local in eastern England.

Red Kite *Milvus milvus* 61–63cm (24–25in) Plumage usually a good deal more rufous than Buzzard, especially tail, while the head is normally paler. **Flight** Long wings and long forked tail are easily seen when the bird soars overhead. A large whitish patch on the underside of the wings is distinctive. When gliding the wings are held level. **Habitat** Hilly country with well-wooded slopes. **Distribution** About twenty-six pairs currently breeding in central Wales, where extensively protected by RSPB, Nature Conservancy Council and others; rarely seen away from that area.

Golden Eagle

Buzzard

Sparrowhawk ♂

♀

Red Kite

Marsh Harrier *Circus aeruginosus* 48–56cm (19–22in) Largest of the harriers with a variable, mainly brown plumage, females, immature males and juveniles having creamy heads and shoulders. **Flight** The heaviest of the three harriers having broad rounded wings, while the adult male has extensive grey on the secondaries and grey tail. Hunts by quartering reedbeds and marshes, normally at no great height. **Habitat** Extensive reedbeds, swamps and marshes; occasionally to nearby cultivated areas. **Distribution** Mainly a rare summer visitor breeding only at a few sites in East Anglia where it may winter; occasionally elsewhere, but seen on passage in other areas. RSPB reserve at Minsmere, Suffolk, is its most regular breeding site (one or two pairs).

Hen Harrier *Circus cyaneus* 43–51cm (17–20in) More slender than Marsh, the sexes being easily distinguished. **Flight** Long, slender, slightly angled wings and long tail, the white rump patch being conspicuous in the female. Has a graceful buoyant action, a few wing-beats then a long shallow glide. **Habitat** Moorland and adjacent valleys including young conifer plantations; in winter moves to lowland heaths, rough pastures, marshes and dunes. **Distribution** Only bird of prey to have really increased its range in recent years. Now breeds in many areas in Scotland, parts of northern England, north Wales and throughout Ireland. In winter moves to other parts of Britain.

Montagu's Harrier *Circus pygargus* 41–46cm (16–18in) Male differs from male Hen by having a dark wing-bar and brown streaks on the belly. Female very similar to female Hen. **Flight** Slimmer wings and more buoyant flight than Hen. Separated from that species by an absence of the white rump in the male and a much smaller rump area in the female, though in the latter this feature is a variable and not clear-cut distinction. **Habitat** Marshes, rough commons, moorlands and large sand-dune areas. **Distribution** Summer visitor; now one of our rarest raptors with a handful of pairs breeding in south-west England and occasionally elsewhere.

Osprey *Pandion haliaetus* (family Pandionidae) 51–58cm (20–23in) Easily distinguished from other large birds of prey by means of its contrasting dark brown upperparts and snow white underparts. **Flight** Long, somewhat narrow, wings having a distinct angle at the carpal joint. When fishing flies at anything up to 30 metres (100 feet) above the water, hovering heavily before plunging after its prey. **Habitat** Lakes and rivers in wooded areas. **Distribution** Summer visitor with less than twenty pairs breeding in the Scottish Highlands after initial establishment at RSPB Loch Garten reserve; elsewhere on passage.

Marsh Harrier

Marsh Harrier

♀

♂

Hen Harrier

Hen Harrier

♀

♂

Montagu's Harrier

Osprey

Falcons family Falconidae

Hobby *Falco subbuteo* 30–36cm (12–14in) Longer winged and shorter tailed than Kestrel, with streaked underparts and rufous thighs. **Flight** Our most agile falcon; the long scythe-like wings and a short tail suggest a large Swift. Feeds on insects as much as birds, often continuing to catch the former until twilight. **Habitat** Downland and heaths with small woodlands; also well-timbered agricultural areas. **Distribution** Summer visitor; about 100 pairs breed in southern England, occasionally elsewhere; otherwise a casual visitor.

Peregrine *Falco peregrinus* 38–48cm (15–19in) Crow-sized, this is our largest breeding falcon. Dark-headed with conspicuous black moustachial stripes. **Flight** Rapid and often somewhat pigeon-like, with winnowing wings which are outspread during frequent lengthy glides. **Habitat** Mainly open country with cliffs or inland crags on which the birds nest; in winter many move to estuaries, marshes and not infrequently inland. **Distribution** Population much reduced during the late 1950s through effects of toxic chemical poisoning; has made some recovery but still not regained its former status. Breeds mainly in the Scottish Highlands, thence down the western side of Great Britain and in parts of Ireland; ranges further afield in winter.

Merlin *Falco columbarius* 27–33cm (10½–13in) Male is much smaller than other falcons and female a good deal browner than female Kestrel with which it might be confused. **Flight** Very dashing, usually low over the ground with frequent changes of direction, catching small birds after swift pursuits. Like the preceding falcons, the Merlin may hover briefly but not habitually like Kestrel. **Habitat** Hills and open moorland, coming to lower ground, saltings and dunes mainly in winter. **Distribution** Breeds mainly in Scotland, northern England and central Wales with a few in south-west England. Winters in all coastal areas.

Kestrel *Falco tinnunculus* 33–36cm (13–14in) Males should not be confused with any other bird of prey, while the longer pointed wings distinguish the female from Sparrowhawk. **Flight** Generally slower than other falcons though with rapid wing-beats; the frequent and lengthy hovering is distinctive. **Habitat** Almost ubiquitous from city centres to open country and the coast. **Distribution** Breeds throughout Great Britain and Ireland.

Hobby

Peregrine juvenile

Peregrine ♂

Merlin ♂ ♀

Kestrel ♀ ♂

Birds of prey and owls in flight. (Birds with the same accompanying symbol are to the same scale. Those without a symbol are not to scale.)

Sparrowhawk ○
♂

Red Kite ○

Buzzard ○

Sparrowhawk ○
♀

Marsh Harrier ♂

Hen Harrier ♂

Montagu's Harrier ♂

Marsh Harrier
♀ juvenile

Hen Harrier
♀ juvenile

Montagu's
Harrier
♀ juvenile

Osprey

Peregrine ♀

Osprey ♀

Osprey

Golden Eagle

Long-eared Owl ♀

Short-eared Owl ♀

Short-eared Owl

Golden Eagle sub-adult

Kestrel

Kestrel ♀

Merlin

Merlin ♀

Grouse family Tetraonidae

Red Grouse *Lagopus lagopus* 32–41 cm (13–16 in) A rather stout bird easily recognizable with its dark red-brown plumage. Possibly confused only with the female Black, though is smaller, redder coloured and has a rounded unforked tail. **Flight** Flies with rapid beats of its short wings interspersed with long glides low over the ground. **Voice** A cackling 'kowk, kok-ok-ok-ok', while the male in display is the source of the well-known moorland sound 'go-bak, bak-bak-bak'. **Habitat** Upland moors where heather is well established. **Distribution** Breeds throughout Scotland and much of northern England and Ireland, parts of Wales, Devon and Cornwall.

Ptarmigan *Lagopus mutus* 32–36 cm (13–14 in) Its white wings distinguish it at all seasons and no other gamebird is completely white in winter. Like other grouse, the Ptarmigan has feathered legs. **Flight** Similar to Red Grouse; often flushed only at the last moment; on landing merges immediately with its surroundings. **Voice** Mainly a harsh croak. **Habitat** Barren areas on or close to mountain tops; even during severe weather moves only to slightly lower ground. **Distribution** Scotland, mainly on mountains over 900 metres (3,000 feet) but lower in some areas, especially in north-west.

Black Grouse *Lyrurus tetrix* male 53 cm (21 in); female 41 cm (16 in) The male can hardly be confused with any other species. Females are browner than Red, while they are smaller and less boldly marked than female Capercaillie. **Flight** Rapid wing-beats; low when amongst cover but rises over open country. **Voice** A sneezing 'tch-sheew', while the male during display has various bubbling notes and females a loud 'chuck-chuk'. **Habitat** Moorland fringes and sparsely wooded heaths, often amongst developing conifer plantations. **Distribution** Scotland, though not extreme north, northern England, parts of Wales, Exmoor and the Quantocks.

Capercaillie *Tetrao urogallus* male 86 cm (34 in); female 62 cm (24 in) Turkey-sized male is unmistakable; females might be confused with female Black Grouse but are larger, have a rufous breast patch and a rounded tail. **Flight** Noisy when breaking cover. Often perches in trees. **Voice** Males mainly silent except during display; females a harsh 'kok-kok'. **Habitat** Mainly mature coniferous woodland but regularly moves to mixed areas in winter. **Distribution** Sedentary, breeding in the eastern Highlands; attempted introduction in north-west England.

Red Grouse

Ptarmigan

♂ winter

♀ autumn

Black Grouse

♂

♀

Capercaillie

♀

♂

Partridges, pheasants family Phasianidae

Red-legged Partridge *Alectoris rufa* 34cm (13½in) Larger than Grey from which it may be distinguished by its white cheeks, throat bordered with black and by its heavily barred flanks. Juveniles are not so prominently marked and are then not unlike juvenile Grey, though have spots rather than streaks. **Flight** Usually prefers to run at the approach of danger, but will fly swiftly when flushed, the flocks — 'coveys' — usually dispersing. **Voice** A harsh 'chuka-chuka'. **Habitat** Fields, heaths and downs. **Distribution** An introduced resident, breeding mainly in central and southern England; also frequently introduced, though with variable success, elsewhere.

Grey Partridge *Perdix perdix* 30cm (12in) Main identification points are the pale chestnut head and grey neck, while males have a conspicuous dark mark on the lower breast. **Flight** Short rounded wings and a rufous tail; usually flies low over the ground. **Voice** A loud grating 'kar-wic'. **Habitat** Chiefly on arable land, but also occurs on heaths, sand-dunes, moorlands and marshes. **Distribution** Breeds throughout most of Great Britain and Ireland; less numerous in the north and west, numbers declining in recent years.

Quail *Coturnix coturnix* 18cm (7in) Rather like a miniature Grey Partridge though of slighter build and a more sandy colour. Sexes rather similar though the female lacks the black throat markings of the male. **Flight** Most reluctant to be flushed, and then only travels for a short distance low over the ground. Much prefers to hide or run from danger. **Voice** The characteristic 'quic-ic-ic', often interpreted as 'wet-my-lips', may be heard during the spring and early summer, often at some distance from the bird and not infrequently at night. Quite often calling birds provide the only indication that this species is present. **Habitat** Rough grasslands and cereal crops. **Distribution** Summer visitor in variable though rarely large numbers to Great Britain and Ireland. Has nested, though rarely annually in many counties, most frequently in southern England, though may do so north to Shetland.

Pheasant *Phasianus colchicus* male 66–89cm (30–35in); female 53–63cm (21–25in) The male is unmistakable with its bright colours and long tail. The browner female has a shorter tail though only immatures may possibly be confused with a partridge. **Flight** Prefers to run for cover; otherwise a noisy take-off, rapid wing-beats and, before landing, a long glide. **Voice** A strident 'karrk-karrk'. **Habitat** Woods and areas of thick cover. **Distribution** Resident, breeding throughout most of Great Britain and Ireland.

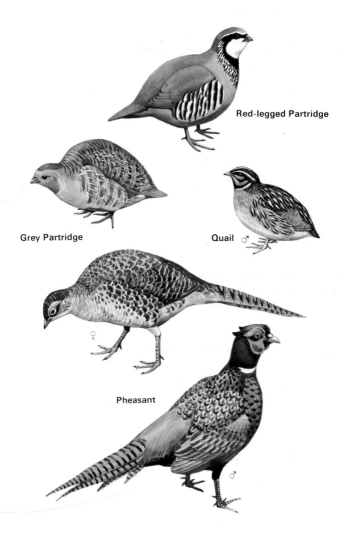

Red-legged Partridge

Grey Partridge

Quail ♂

Pheasant ♀

Pheasant ♂

Crakes, rails, Coot family Rallidae

Water Rail *Rallus aquaticus* 28cm (11in) A secretive species but when visible the long red bill is an excellent identification feature. Whitish undertail coverts, not so conspicuous as in Moorhen. Olive brown upperparts and black and white flanks. **Flight** Weak and fluttering with dangling legs and usually of only short duration. **Voice** A variety of groans, grunts and squeaks, together with a persistent 'gep-gep' call. Often heard after dark. **Habitat** Reedbeds, swampy margins of ponds, rivers and overgrown ditches. **Distribution** Main breeding areas are in East Anglia and in Ireland; more scattered in other areas but is probably overlooked. More widespread in winter when immigration takes place.

Corncrake *Crex crex* 27cm (10½in) Rather like a small slender gamebird, though rarely seen until flushed. Yellowish buff and well-marked upperparts. **Flight** Will run away when disturbed but when flushed its chestnut wings, dangling legs and sluggish flight distinguish it from partridges and Quail. **Voice** A rasping continuous 'crek-crek' which may be heard at night as much as during the day. Can be imitated by striking a piece of wood across a comb which may on occasions attract a bird close to the observer. **Habitat** Mainly lush grasslands. **Distribution** Summer visitor, now only breeding regularly in parts of northern England, western Scotland and Ireland; sporadic elsewhere, though regularly encountered on passage when calling birds may remain for some days.

Moorhen *Gallinula chloropus* 33cm (13in) One of our best known waterside birds. Adults and young continually flirt tail to show conspicuous white undertail coverts. **Flight** Rather laboured with legs either dangling or projecting behind the tail; usually prefers to run for cover. **Voice** A loud 'kr-r-rk' or 'kittac'. **Habitat** All waterside areas with cover. **Distribution** Breeds widely throughout Great Britain and Ireland.

Coot *Fulica atra* 38cm (15in) Stoutly built with a white frontal shield and bill. Often in large flocks and generally very quarrelsome. **Flight** Patters along the surface before taking off, feet outstretched once airborne. **Voice** A high pitched 'kowk'. **Habitat** Requires larger, more open waters than Moorhen, and in winter may visit estuaries and sheltered bays during hard weather. **Distribution** Resident breeding throughout much of Great Britain and Ireland, numbers being augmented in winter by continental immigrants.

Water Rail

Corncrake

Moorhen

Coot

Waders

Oystercatcher *Haematopus ostralegus* (family Haematopodidae) 43cm (17in) One of our most conspicuous and easily recognizable waders. having pied plumage, an orange-red bill and red legs. **Flight** Flies with shallow wing-beats. **Voice** A noisy 'kleep-kleep'. **Habitat** Found mainly along coast and on estuaries; extends to lakes, rivers and moorland in northern districts. **Distribution** Resident, breeding on virtually all coasts and inland from the Pennines northwards.

Lapwing *Vanellus vanellus* (family Charadriidae) 30cm (12in) our only wader to support a crest which, when viewed at close quarters, can be clearly seen as metallic green as are the upperparts. **Flight** Broad, rounded wings and leisurely, often erratic, flight. **Voice** A wheezy 'kee-wi'. **Habitat** Breeds mainly on agricultural areas; many move in winter to estuary regions. **Distribution** Breeds throughout Great Britain and Ireland with a considerable winter immigration.

Ringed Plover *Charadrius hiaticula* 19cm (7½in) One of the smaller waders, robustly built and with a short bill. Usually very active. **Flight** Rapid and low. **Voice** A liquid 'too-li'. **Habitat** Breeds mainly along the shore where it is currently decreasing due to disturbance; also inland in the north. **Distribution** Breeds on all coasts apart from the south-west of England; inland in parts of Scotland, Ireland and East Anglia. More numerous in winter.

Little Ringed Plover *Charadrius dubius* 15cm (6in) Difficult to tell from Ringed Plover though has a white line on the forehead, flesh-coloured legs, no wing-bar in flight. **Voice** 'Pee-u'. **Habitat** Gravel pits, rivers and lakes. **Distribution** Summer visitor, extending its range through south and central England.

Grey Plover *Pluvialis squatarola* 28cm (11in) Though migrants may be in breeding plumage, mainly seen in winter plumage when uniform grey colour distinguishes it from Golden Plover. **Flight** Conspicuous black axillaries. **Voice** High-pitched 'tlee-oo-ee'. **Habitat** Estuaries. **Distribution** Passage migrant and winter visitor.

Golden Plover *Pluvialis apricaria* 28cm (11in) Has distinctive black and gold spangled upperparts; browner in winter when throat and underparts lack black markings. **Flight** Rapid, often in compact flocks. **Voice** A liquid 'tlui'. **Habitat** Breeds on moorland, moving to lower agricultural land in winter. Regular on coast in some areas. **Distribution** Breeds mainly from the southern Pennines northwards; rather few in Wales and Ireland, but winters in all districts.

Oystercatcher

Lapwing

Little Ringed Plover

Ringed Plover

summer

winter

Grey Plover

summer

winter

Golden Plover

Dotterel *Eudromias morinellus* 22 cm (8½ in) A rather striking wader in summer plumage; greyish brown on autumn passage though retaining the prominent eye-stripes and pectoral band. Often very tame. **Flight** Similar to Golden Plover. **Voice** A trilling 'wit-e-wee'. **Habitat** Breeds on barren mountains above 780 metres (2,500 feet). Passage birds occur on pastures, heaths and marshes while in the Netherlands it breeds on arable land. **Distribution** Summer visitor in small numbers breeding in the central Highlands; occasionally elsewhere.

Turnstone *Arenaria interpres* 23 cm (9 in) Basically a black and white stocky, short-billed wader; upperparts considerably brighter in summer but even then inconspicuous among rocks, pebbles and seaweed. **Flight** Takes flight reluctantly and usually flies for only a short distance somewhat slowly. **Voice** A twittering 'kitititit'. **Habitat** Rocky or pebble shores; in sandy estuaries only where weed-covered reefs occur. **Distribution** Mainly a winter visitor to all coasts though non-breeders summer in many areas.

Snipe *Gallinago gallinago* (family Scolopacidae) 27 cm (10½ in) The brown plumage and secretive habits of this species mean that it is rarely seen until flushed from cover. **Flight** When flushed zig-zags away and often 'towers' the long bill often being easily visible. **Voice** Spring note a persistent 'chick-ka', while during display flights the well-known 'drumming' may be heard. This is made as the bird dives about the sky, the outer tail feathers producing short bursts of vibrations. When flushed the birds repeatedly make a harsh 'krepe'. **Habitat** Boggy areas with good cover. **Distribution** Resident breeding throughout much of Great Britain and Ireland.

Jack Snipe *Lymnocryptes minimus* 19 cm (7½ in) Like a miniature Snipe, but has a relatively shorter bill. Difficult to observe. **Flight** Rises from ground at last minute and instead of towering usually drops again within a few yards. **Voice** Normally silent except for an occasional weak 'skaap'. **Habitat** Marshy areas. **Distribution** Winter visitor, usually in small numbers to all areas.

Woodcock *Scolopax rusticola* 34 cm (13½ in) Like a big, stocky Snipe, usually flushed in woodland. Has mainly crepuscular habits. **Flight** Rises noisily and dodges rapidly away. The 'roding' display is a circuit of slow, rather owl-like wingbeats, usually just above the trees. **Voice** Males when 'roding' have a characteristic 'si-wick' note and a quiet double grunting note; otherwise mainly silent. **Habitat** Damp woodlands. **Distribution** Breeds throughout much of Great Britain and Ireland with immigration taking place each autumn from the Continent, so that in some areas it may be locally abundant.

summer   winter   summer

Dotterel   **Turnstone**

Snipe

Jack Snipe

Woodcock

Curlew *Numenius arquata* 48–64 cm (19–25 in) The largest wader with long legs, a long down-curved bill and buffish brown streaked plumage. **Flight** Takes off at the slightest hint of danger or disturbance and flies strongly with regular, rather gull-like wing-beats. **Voice** Varied, but the loud 'coorwee coorwee' notes are familiar in many areas. Also has a series of liquid bubbling notes heard mainly in spring. **Habitat** Breeds mainly in upland areas though does occur at lower altitudes when it chooses wet meadows, heaths and even dunes. Winters mainly on estuaries but also inland on wet meadows. **Distribution** Breeds throughout much of Great Britain and Ireland except for south-east England; common visitor to all estuary areas in winter.

Whimbrel *Numenius phaeopus* 38–41 cm (15–16 in) Like rather small Curlew with relatively shorter bill. When seen at fairly close range its head pattern is distinctive. **Flight** More rapid wing-beats than Curlew. **Voice** The best distinguishing feature from its larger relative, the main call being a tittering 'titti-titti-titti'; also has a bubbling Curlew-like song. **Habitat** Breeds on moorlands; passage birds occur mainly on estuaries, sometimes on rocky shores. **Distribution** Summer visitor, breeding in Orkney and Shetland with a few pairs in the north Highlands; elsewhere occurs on passage with a few overwintering.

Black-tailed Godwit *Limosa limosa* 38–43 cm (15–17 in) A tall, slender wading bird with long legs and a long straight bill. In summer the head, neck and breast are bright chestnut, with blackish markings on both upper and underparts. **Flight** Feet project noticeably beyond tail while the broad white wing-bar and bold tail pattern distinguish it from the other large waders, with which it might be confused. **Voice** A loud 'wicka-wicka' heard in flight. **Habitat** In breeding season mainly rough damp pastures, water meadows and the like. Estuaries and nearby areas in winter, but also visits freshwater marshes, sewage farms and reservoir margins. **Distribution** One regular breeding site in Cambridgeshire, especially at RSPB Ouse Washes reserve; sporadic elsewhere. Frequent on passage elsewhere with many wintering, particularly in the south.

Bar-tailed Godwit *Limosa lapponica* 35–38 cm (14–15 in) Very similar to Black-tailed, but shorter legs, slightly upturned bill and in summer the whole of the underparts chestnut-red. In winter plumage not unlike that of Curlew. **Flight** Feet project only slightly beyond tail; rump whitish and no wing-bar. **Voice** 'Kirruc-kirruc'. **Habitat** Sandy shores and estuaries; rare inland. **Distribution** Mainly a passage and winter visitor to all coasts; a few summer.

Curlew

Whimbrel

winter

Bar-tailed Godwit

summer

winter

Black-tailed Godwit

Green Sandpiper *Tringa ochropus* 23cm (9in) A shy bird with dark upperparts, conspicuous white rump and greenish legs. **Flight** When flushed looks not unlike large House Martin and usually adopts a towering erratic flight with jerky, rather Snipe-like wing-beats. **Voice** A ringing 'weet-a-weet'. **Habitat** Occurs beside lakes, ponds, ditches and estuary gutters, usually where there is shelter. **Distribution** Mainly a passage migrant to England, Wales and eastern Scotland; rather few elsewhere. A few overwinter.

Wood Sandpiper *Tringa glareola* 20cm (8in) Plumage at rest and in flight does not have the contrast of Green Sandpiper, being paler above. **Flight** Shows white rump and feet project beyond tail, but does not look so 'black-and-white' as Green Sandpiper. **Voice** An excited 'chiff-iff'. **Habitat** Breeds in swampy woodlands; on passage visits small pools, creeks, sewage farms and lake margins. **Distribution** A few pairs now breed in north-east Scotland; otherwise seen on passage, mainly in south-east.

Common Sandpiper *Tringa hypoleucos* 20cm (7$\frac{3}{4}$in) A small slender wader with a rather horizontal stance and continual bobbing action. **Flight** Usually low with rapid but shallow wing-beats and frequent glides. **Voice** When flushed a piping 'twee-ee-ee'. **Habitat** Breeds close to the gravel banks of lakes and rivers, chiefly in upland districts. On passage occurs widely inland and often at coast. **Distribution** Breeds mainly in northern and western Britain, though no further south than mid-Wales. Passage birds encountered almost anywhere, with a few over-wintering.

Redshank *Tringa totanus* 28cm (11in) A brown wader with a medium length bill and striking orange-red legs. **Flight** White hind edge of wings and white rump conspicuous. **Voice** Noisy; alarm call a loud 'tew-hee-hee'. **Habitat** Breeds on grassy meadows, coastal saltings and low moorlands; otherwise very much an estuarine species. **Distribution** Resident, breeding in most counties.

Spotted Redshank *Tringa erythropus* 30cm (12in) In summer its mainly black plumage is unmistakable. In winter, a pale bird, more slender than Redshank; white rump but no wing markings. **Flight** Strong though erratic, with projecting legs. **Voice** A clear 'tchu-it'. **Habitat** Coastal areas and inland pools. **Distribution** Mainly an autumn passage migrant, though some seen midsummer while others overwinter.

Greenshank *Tringa nebularia* 30cm (12in) A tall grey-white wader with a long, slightly upturned bill. **Flight** No wing markings, conspicuous white rump extending up the lower back. **Voice** A loud 'tew-ew-tew'. **Habitat** Breeds on moorland with pools; winters on estuaries. **Distribution** Breeds in the north-west Highlands; elsewhere a passage migrant and winter visitor.

Green Sandpiper

Wood Sandpiper

Common Sandpiper

Redshank

Greenshank
winter

Spotted Redshank
winter

Knot *Calidris canutus* 25cm (10in) A greyish, short-billed wader midway in size between Redshank and Dunlin; of stocky build with a short neck. May show reddish underparts in spring and autumn. **Flight** Often in large compact flocks. Has a rather indistinct pale wing-bar and a pale rump and tail. **Voice** In flight a mellow 'twit-wit'. **Habitat** Mainly estuaries. **Distribution** Passage migrant and winter visitor, occasional in summer.

Purple Sandpiper *Calidris maritima* 21cm (8¼in) Slightly larger and darker than Dunlin, its short yellow legs providing a rather portly appearance. **Flight** Swift, direct and usually of short duration. **Voice** Generally silent, though when flushed has a piping 'wee-it'. **Habitat** Rocky shores, weed covered piers and groynes. **Distribution** Passage migrant and winter visitor to rocky coasts.

Little Stint *Calidris minuta* 13cm (5¼in) One of our smallest waders; rather like miniature Dunlin but with short, straight bill. **Flight** Rapid, its narrow wing-bar not conspicuous. **Voice** A sharp 'chik'. **Habitat** Estuaries and not infrequently inland at reservoirs, sewage farms and lakes. **Distribution** Passage migrant, mainly in autumn, chiefly on the east coast.

Dunlin *Calidris alpina* 16–19cm (6¾–7½in) Our commonest and most numerous small wader with a long, slightly down-curved bill. The black belly patch is conspicuous in summer. **Flight** Usually in flocks which wheel and twist, the birds in complete unison, first with white undersides showing, then darker upperparts. **Voice** A weak 'treap'. **Habitat** Breeds on moorland with pools and boggy areas; mainly on estuaries in winter but small numbers at inland waters. **Distribution** Breeds in Scotland and northern England, sparingly in Wales and Ireland; elsewhere a numerous passage and winter visitor.

Curlew Sandpiper *Calidris ferruginea* 19cm (7½in) In winter plumage looks like slender Dunlin, but has a paler breast, brighter eye-stripe and a more slender down-curved bill. **Flight** Similar to Dunlin and has the same wing-bar, but unlike that species the rump is distinctly white. **Voice** A soft 'chirrip'. **Habitat** Estuaries and sometimes inland. **Distribution** Mainly a passage migrant; more numerous in autumn and chiefly on the east coast.

Sanderling *Calidris alba* 20cm (8in) A very active bird, almost ceaseless in its movements. Virtually white in winter plumage. Bill stouter and shorter than in Dunlin. **Flight** Reluctant to take off but when it does so shows a bright white wing-bar. **Voice** A liquid 'quit quit'. **Habitat** Sandy shores. **Distribution** Passage migrant but also winters on most coasts.

summer

winter

Knot

Purple Sandpiper

Little Stint

winter

summer

Dunlin

summer

winter

Curlew Sandpiper

Sanderling
winter

Ruff *Philomachus pugnax* male 28–30 cm (11–12 in) ; female 22–25 cm (8½–10 in) Only males in summer show the full breeding plumage ; otherwise both sexes and immatures look rather nondescript and vary considerably in size and colour of legs. **Flight** Somewhat like that of Redshank. The oval white patch on each side of the otherwise dark tail is a good feature. **Voice** A low 'tu-whit'. **Habitat** Ouse Washes, water meadows, including RSPB reserve, are only known breeding grounds. On passage visits the shores of lakes, gravel pits and sewage farms, rather infrequent on estuaries. **Distribution** Breeds at one site in Cambridgeshire ; otherwise a passage or winter visitor, most numerous in eastern districts.

Avocet *Recurvirostra avosetta* (family Recurvirostridae) 43 cm (17 in) One of our most unmistakable birds with a long, 9·3 cm (3¾ in), upturned bill. **Flight** Black and white pattern conspicuous as are the long bill and feet projecting well beyond the tail. **Voice** Noisy, particularly at the nest ; main call a clear 'klooit'. **Habitat** Breeds beside shallow brackish lagoons ; winters on estuaries. **Distribution** Summer visitor, almost all breeding at RSPB reserves at Havergate and Minsmere, Suffolk. Some birds regularly winter in south-west England ; otherwise only seen on passage, rather rarely in most districts.

Grey Phalarope *Phalaropus fulicarius* (family Phalaropodidae) 20·5 cm (8 in) Phalaropes are the only waders which regularly swim which they do buoyantly, looking like miniature gulls. May often be seen spinning on the surface, eating invertebrates brought up by this action. **Flight** Most reluctant to take off and over short distances rather weak and erratic. **Voice** A soft 'twit'. **Habitat** Mainly at sea ; occasionally on inland waters. **Distribution** Passage migrant, chiefly in autumn.

Red-necked Phalarope *Phalaropus lobatus* 17 cm (6½ in) In summer the female is much brighter coloured than the male. Distinguished in winter from Grey by its smaller size, more slender bill and darker back with white markings. **Flight** Similar to Grey. **Voice** A low-pitched 'whit'. **Habitat** Breeds on marshy ground near open water. **Distribution** Summer visitor, breeding in small numbers in north and north-west Scotland with a single colony in Ireland. Elsewhere a scarce passage migrant.

Stone Curlew *Burhinus oedicnemus* (family Burhinidae) 41 cm (16 in) A large round-headed bird having streaked sandy plumage, yellow eyes and legs. **Flight** Rather slow wing-beats with trailing legs ; two whitish wing-bars. **Voice** Shrill and Curlew-like. **Habitat** Sandy heaths, waste land and chalk uplands. **Distribution** Summer visitor, breeding sparsely in several south-eastern counties ; rarely seen elsewhere.

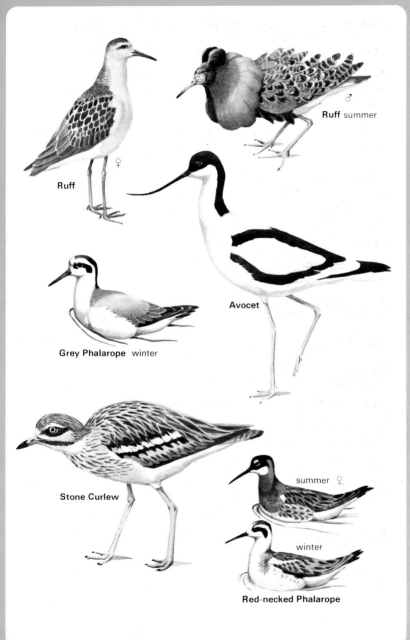

Ruff summer ♂

Ruff ♀

Grey Phalarope winter

Avocet

Stone Curlew

summer ♀

winter

Red-necked Phalarope

Waders in flight. (Birds with the same accompanying symbol are to the same scale. Those without a symbol are not to scale.)

Lapwing ○

Woodcock ○

Avocet ○

Oystercatcher ○

Lapwing ○

Dotterel
winter □

Grey Plover
winter □

Golden Plover
winter □

Black-tailed
Godwit
winter □

Stone
Curlew □

Bar-tailed Godwit
winter □

Jack Snipe ◇

Curlew □

Whimbrel □

Snipe ◇

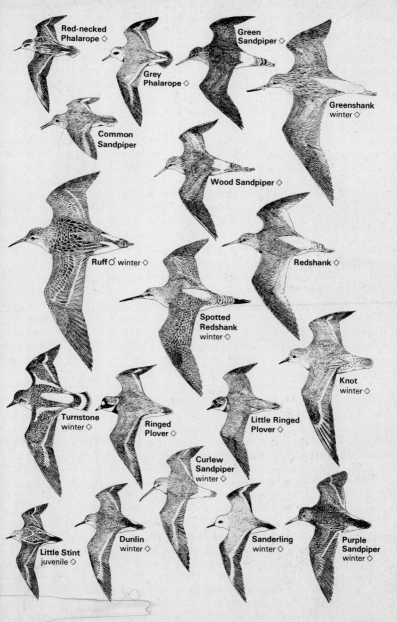

Red-necked Phalarope ◇

Grey Phalarope ◇

Green Sandpiper ◇

Greenshank winter ◇

Common Sandpiper

Wood Sandpiper ◇

Ruff ♂ winter ◇

Redshank ◇

Spotted Redshank winter ◇

Knot winter ◇

Turnstone winter ◇

Ringed Plover ◇

Little Ringed Plover ◇

Curlew Sandpiper winter ◇

Little Stint juvenile ◇

Dunlin winter ◇

Sanderling winter ◇

Purple Sandpiper winter ◇

Skuas family Stercorariidae

Great Skua *Stercorarius skua* 58cm (23in) Much stockier built than rather similar sized Herring Gull, and much darker plumaged than immatures of that species. **Flight** Heavier than a gull but surprisingly swift when pursuing other birds or at the breeding grounds. Large and conspicuous white wing-patches. **Voice** A loud 'hah-hah-hah-hah' heard at the breeding colonies. **Habitat** Maritime except in breeding season when it comes to moorland and rough pasture on islands, and occasionally mainland areas. **Distribution** Breeds in Shetland and Orkney with small numbers in the Outer Hebrides and the north mainland of Scotland. Regular on passage elsewhere, mainly in the autumn.

Arctic Skua *Stercorarius parasiticus* 43–47cm (17–18½in) Much more slender built than Great and, unlike that species, occurs in two colour phases together with a variety of intermediates. The central tail feathers are not elongated in immatures. **Flight** Graceful and hawk-like. Very agile when pursuing other seabirds, like the Kittiwake and terns, in order to force them to drop or disgorge their last meal on which it then feeds. **Voice** A wailing 'ki-aow' at the breeding colonies. **Habitat** Similar to Great. **Distribution** Similar to Great though some breed south to the Inner Hebrides. Seen off most coasts in autumn as the birds move south.

Gulls and terns family Laridae

Great Black-backed Gull *Larus marinus* 64–69cm (25–27in) Our largest gull, only possibly confused with smaller Lesser Black-backed which has slate, not a black mantle and wings, and yellow not flesh coloured legs. **Flight** Powerful. **Voice** A barking 'aouk'. **Habitat** Rocky coasts and islands; occasionally inland for breeding. Visits estuaries, lakes and rivers in winter. **Distribution** Breeds around much of Great Britain and Ireland except for the east coast between the Forth and the Isle of Wight; more widespread in winter with immigration from the continent.

Lesser Black-backed Gull *Larus fuscus* 53cm (21in) Smaller and more slender built than Great Black-backed. **Flight** Powerful, usually with much gliding. **Voice** A loud 'kiaow-kiaow'. **Habitat** Breeds on islands, occasionally on the mainland coast and not infrequently on inland moors, sometimes in huge colonies. **Distribution** Mainly a summer visitor, mostly breeding in the west and north; passage visitor elsewhere with many more now wintering.

Great Skua

Arctic Skua
dark phase

Arctic Skua
light phase

Lesser Black-backed Gull

Great Black-backed Gull

Herring Gull *Larus argentatus* 56cm (22in) The same size as Lesser Black-backed but more stockily built; immatures cannot be separated in their first year or so. **Flight** Powerful, the bird being a master glider in up-draughts above cliffs or when following a ship. **Voice** Varied, but a loud 'kyow-kyow' is most frequently used. **Habitat** Catholic, breeding almost as frequently on low shores as on cliffs; some inland colonies while others nest on roof-tops in coastal towns. Frequent visitor to inland areas and is readily attracted to rubbish dumps, poultry farms and the like. **Distribution** Resident, breeding on virtually all coasts with the smallest numbers in south-east England.

Common Gull *Larus canus* 41cm (16in) Rather like a small Herring, but size differences immediately apparent when the two are seen together. Bill shorter and less stout with no red spot near the tip. Legs greenish yellow in contrast to the flesh colour of the larger species. **Flight** Similar to Herring. **Voice** A shrill mewing 'kee-ya'. **Habitat** Breeds mainly inland on moorlands and on islands in lakes. When on the coast it usually chooses fairly level ground but can also be discovered on steep grassy slopes. **Distribution** Breeds mainly in Scotland and Ireland with a handful of pairs in England and Wales. Numerous winter visitor to all areas.

Black-headed Gull *Larus ridibundus* 35–38cm (14–15in) Adults in summer plumage with their chocolate brown hood are unmistakable; the red bill and legs are also conspicuous. In late summer the hood is lost, apart from a dark smudge behind the eye, and not regained until the following spring. **Flight** Buoyant and in all plumages a pure white leading edge to the wing is visible. **Voice** A harsh 'kwarr'. **Habitat** Breeds at a variety of inland sites—gravel pits, sewage farms and pools—while on the coast low islands and the fringes of lagoons are chosen. In winter ranges widely inland while it is also numerous on estuaries and sheltered coasts. **Distribution** Breeds throughout much of Great Britain and Ireland, some colonies having long histories while others are short-lived due to habitat changes. More widely distributed in winter.

Kittiwake *Rissa tridactyla* 41cm (16in) At first glance rather like a more slender Common Gull, but has much shorter black legs. **Flight** Buoyant, at times swift, the black wing-tips lack the white spots of some other gulls. **Voice** A screaming 'kitt-ee-wake'. **Habitat** Breeds mainly on sea cliffs though harbour walls and warehouses used in a few areas. **Distribution** Breeds on most suitable coastlines, dispersing out to sea in winter.

Herring Gull summer

Herring Gull winter

Herring Gull juvenile

Common Gull

winter

summer

Black-headed Gull

adult

juvenile

Kittiwake

Black Tern *Chlidonias niger* 24cm (9½in) Unmistakable in summer plumage; in winter the forehead, neck and underparts are white with a dark 'shoulder' mark extending from the wings. **Flight** Buoyant, frequently hovering just above the water surface. **Voice** A squeaky 'kik-kik'. **Habitat** In breeding season wet marshes and fens; frequents inland waters as well as the coast when on passage. **Distribution** Summer visitor, breeding only in Cambridgeshire, but regular on passage north to central Scotland.

Common Tern *Sterna hirundo* 35cm (14in) One of our most graceful seabirds having long wings and tail streamers. In summer the orange-red bill has a distinct, though variable black tip. **Flight** Buoyant, but has deliberate wing-beats. **Voice** A high-pitched 'kee-yah'. **Habitat** Breeds on shingle banks, coastal lagoons and inland on rivers, lakes and gravel pits. **Distribution** Summer visitor, breeding mainly in southern areas, though virtually none in south-west England and south Wales.

Arctic Tern *Sterna paradisaea* 35cm (14in) Very similar to Common, though the black tip is absent or much reduced on the blood red bill. **Flight** Similar to Common. **Voice** A whistling 'kee-kee'. **Habitat** Coastal with rather few breeding any distance inland. **Distribution** Breeds mainly in northern England, Scotland and Ireland; regular elsewhere on passage.

Roseate Tern *Sterna dougallii* 38cm (15in) Much whiter plumage and longer tail streamers than the previous two species. **Flight** Extremely buoyant with shallow wing-beats. **Voice** A gutteral 'aaak'. **Habitat** Breeds only on the coast, generally choosing rocky islets. **Distribution** Breeds at a limited number of colonies mainly around the Irish Sea; also in north-east England and eastern Scotland. Rare on passage elsewhere though probably overlooked.

Little Tern *Sterna albifrons* 23–25cm (9–10in) Our smallest tern and the only one having yellow legs and a black-tipped yellow bill. **Flight** Rapid wing-beats. **Voice** A rasping 'kik-kik' or 'kyik'. **Habitat** Breeds mainly on open beaches rarely occurring inland. **Distribution.** Summer visitor, breeding on most suitable coasts with the greatest number in south-east England.

Sandwich Tern *Sterna sandvicensis* 38–43cm (15–17in) Heavier built than other terns. **Flight** More gull-like than other terns. **Voice** A grating 'kirrick'. **Habitat** Breeds on sand-dunes, saltings and shingle. **Distribution** Summer visitor, breeding at a scattering of colonies on most coasts.

Black Tern
summer

Black Tern
winter

Common Tern
summer

Common Tern
winter

Arctic Tern

Roseate Tern

Sandwich Tern

Little Tern

Fulmar *Fulmarus glacialis* (family Procellariidae) 47 cm (18½ in) Rather gull-like but with a more stocky build, large head, thick neck and yellow bill with characteristic tubed nostril at its base. Ungainly on land, rarely leaving the vicinity of the nest. **Flight** Wings narrower than a gull's, not angled and lacking the black tips. Glides over the sea occasionally beating wings for a few yards. Soars in the up-draught along cliff faces. **Voice** Various chuckling and cackling sounds. **Habitat** Pelagic, coming ashore to breed, mainly on cliff coasts. **Distribution** Breeds virtually all round the coast of Great Britain where there are suitable sites. Absent from its nest sites only during the late autumn and early winter.

Auks family Alcidae

Razorbill *Alca torda* 41 cm (16 in) Black upperparts; broad bill and stocky build. Throat and cheeks are white in winter and in immature plumages. **Flight** Fast with rapidly whirring wings, usually low over the sea. **Voice** A growling 'aaarr'. **Habitat** Breeds on cliff coasts, usually amongst boulder scree or on broken cliffs. **Distribution** Breeding colonies situated irregularly along most suitable coastlines. In late autumn birds leave colonies, but many remain in inshore waters throughout the winter.

Guillemot *Uria aalge* 42 cm (16½ in) More slender than Razorbill. A 'bridled' form occurs in small numbers and breeds with normal form. **Flight** Flies fast with whirring wings. **Voice** A trumpeting 'arrra'. **Habitat** Breeds on cliff coasts; in suitable areas immense colonies have been established. **Distribution** Similar to Razorbill; the largest colonies are in Scotland. A dispersal through inshore waters during the winter with birds returning sporadically to the colonies from November onwards.

Black Guillemot *Cepphus grylle* 34 cm (13½ in) When on land adopts a sloping rather than an upright stance. **Flight** Similar to Guillemot. **Voice** A thin reedy 'peeeeee'. **Habitat** Low rocky coasts with caves, crevices and boulders among which the birds nest, never in large colonies. **Distribution** Resident breeding from Shetland southwards to the Solway, but normally not south of the Moray Firth on the east coast. Well distributed in Ireland and the Isle of Man with a few pairs in north-west England and north Wales.

Puffin *Fratercula arctica* 30 cm (12 in) Easily distinguished by large and brightly coloured bills. Immatures have a small grey bill. **Flight** Dumpy outline and rapid wing-beats. **Voice** At the colonies a growling 'aarr'. **Habitat** Breeds mainly on remote islands and inaccessible mainland cliffs with steep grass slopes. **Distribution** Summer visitor to northern and western coasts.

Fulmar

Razorbill

bridled form

summer

winter

Black Guillemot

Guillemot

Puffin

Seabirds in flight. (Birds with the same accompanying symbol are to the same scale. Those without a symbol are not to scale.)

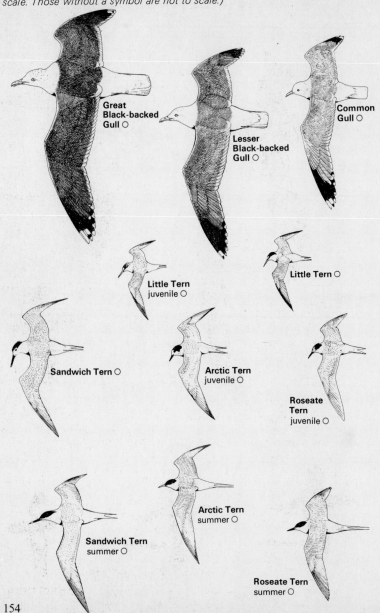

Great Black-backed Gull ○

Lesser Black-backed Gull ○

Common Gull ○

Little Tern juvenile ○

Little Tern ○

Sandwich Tern ○

Arctic Tern juvenile ○

Roseate Tern juvenile ○

Sandwich Tern summer ○

Arctic Tern summer ○

Roseate Tern summer ○

Gannet juvenile ○

Gannet sub-adult ○

Cormorant

Shag

Razorbill ○

Guillemot ○

Black Guillemot ○

155

Doves, pigeons family Columbidae

Stock Dove *Columba oenas* 33cm (13in) Smaller and darker than Woodpigeon and lacking any white markings. **Flight** Rapid, the grey rump and two broken black wing-bars being noticeable. **Voice** A gruff 'oo-roo-oo'. **Habitat** Breeds in holes in trees, particularly old timber; also ruins, cliffs and crags, not infrequently in old rabbit burrows. Feeds on open ground. **Distribution** Resident, breeding north to central and eastern Scotland.

Rock Dove *Columba livia* 33cm (13in) Similar to Stock but easily distinguished on the wing. **Flight** Has a striking white rump. **Voice** 'Oo-roo-coo'. **Habitat** Rocky coasts with caves. **Distribution** Occurs only in isolated western and northern areas; elsewhere the population has been much infiltrated by domestic stock. Feral birds often closely resemble the original wild type.

Woodpigeon *Columba palumbus* 41cm (16in) Our largest pigeon, adults having a conspicuous white neck patch bordered with glossy green. **Flight** Dashes away noisily when flushed showing a broad white wing-band. **Voice** 'Coo-coo-coo'. **Habitat** Chiefly in agricultural areas with numerous trees; also occurs in the urban zone and in some coastal districts. **Distribution** Resident, occurs in all areas.

Turtle Dove *Streptopelia turtur* 27cm (11in) Strikingly rufous upperparts with a black tail edged with white; a black and white patch on the side of the neck. **Flight** Rather flicking wing-beats while the black tail edged white easily discerned. Noticeably pale underparts. **Voice** A purring 'roor-rrr'. **Habitat** Woodlands, copses, large gardens and thick hedgerows. **Distribution** Summer visitor, breeding mainly in the south, but occurs regularly on passage elsewhere.

Collared Dove *Streptopelia decaocto* 32cm (12$\frac{1}{2}$in) Much more uniformly coloured than smaller Turtle, and has a narrow black half-collar. **Flight** Direct and swift. **Voice** A noisy 'coo-cooooo-coo'. **Habitat** Usually close to human habitation, especially where there are tall trees for nesting. **Distribution** Resident, now breeding throughout much of Great Britain and Ireland.

Cuckoo *Cuculus canorus* (family Cuculidae) 33cm (13in) A grey, slender built bird with a long tail. **Flight** Usually low and hurried and terminating in a long glide. Looks not unlike small hawk or falcon. Wings pointed. **Voice** Unmistakable call of the male; females have a bubbling chuckle. **Habitat** Varies from woodlands to moorland and treeless islands. **Distribution** Summer visitor, arriving during late April and breeding throughout Great Britain and Ireland.

Stock Dove

Rock Dove

Woodpigeon

Turtle Dove

Collared Dove

Cuckoo

Owls families Tytonidae and Strigidae

Barn Owl *Tyto alba* 34 cm (13½ in) A pale owl which in the half light at dusk, or when seen briefly in car headlights, looks all-white. **Flight** Slow flapping, at times wavering on rounded wings. **Voice** Wild shrieks, various hissing and snoring noises. **Habitat** Usually agricultural country, but may occur in other open country. **Distribution** Breeds in small numbers in most areas, though not north-west Scotland.

Snowy Owl *Nyctea scandiaca* 53–60 cm (21–24 in) Unmistakable with its huge size, white plumage with variable brown or blackish bars. **Flight** Chiefly diurnal; more Buzzard- than owl-like with frequent glides. **Voice** Normally silent except when breeding. **Habitat** Moorland with rocky knolls. **Distribution** Breeds only on RSPB reserve at Fetlar (Shetlands), but birds seen in summer in several other northern areas. Occasionally wanders further south, especially in winter.

Little Owl *Athene noctua* 22 cm (8½ in) Small size and rather squat flat-headed appearance with bright yellow eyes. Has frequent bobbing action and regularly hunts by day. **Flight** Low, rapid with deep undulations. **Habitat** Varied, but usually in timbered agricultural areas. **Distribution** Resident, breeding north to the border counties; absent other than as a vagrant in Ireland.

Tawny Owl *Strix aluco* 38 cm (15 in) Mainly nocturnal and usually only seen by day at a roosting place where its black eyes and lack of ear-tufts prevent confusion with Long-eared. **Flight** Large head and broad, rounded wings prominent. **Voice** Familiar hooting 'song' and a loud 'kee-wick'. **Habitat** Mainly woodland areas including city parks. **Distribution** Resident, breeding throughout Great Britain except the far north-west and in Ireland.

Long-eared Owl *Asio otus* 45 cm (13½ in) Nocturnal, seldom seen except at regular winter roosts. Has a slim shape, orange eyes and elongated 'ear' tufts. **Flight** Wings and tail longer than Tawny. **Voice** A low 'oo-oo-oo'. **Habitat** Woodland, especially conifers, but hunts in open country. **Distribution** Widely distributed, though local in all areas including Ireland.

Short-eared Owl *Asio flammeus* 38 cm (15 in) Regularly hunts by day, and when at rest adopts a slanting rather than upright inclination. **Flight** Long wings and rather harrier-like movements. **Habitat** Open country. **Distribution** Resident, breeding mainly in northern and western England; a few pairs in eastern districts and throughout Scotland. Regular in winter on the coast elsewhere.

Barn Owl

Snowy Owl

Little Owl

Tawny Owl

Long-eared Owl

Short-eared Owl

Nightjar *Caprimulgus europaeus* (family Caprimulgidae) 27cm (10½in) Crepuscular and rarely seen by day, its finely patterned plumage being an excellent woodland floor camouflage. **Flight** Light, floating, with acrobatic dashes after flying insects. White wing-patches on male. **Voice** A loud nocturnal 'churring'. **Habitat** Woodland, bracken hillsides, dunes and moorland. **Distribution** Decreasing summer visitor, widespread but local.

Swift *Apus apus* (family Apodidae) 16·5cm (6½in) Long scythe-like wings and dark plumage distinguish it from swallows. **Flight** Vigorous and wheeling. **Voice** Mainly a loud screaming. **Habitat** Encountered in all types of habitat but for breeding requires holes in buildings; occasionally cliff crevices. **Distribution** Summer visitor in most areas.

Kingfisher *Alcedo atthis* (family Alcedinidae) 16·5cm (6½in) Unmistakable bright plumage. **Flight** Rapid and usually low. Hovers when fishing. **Voice** A piping 'chee'. **Habitat** Mainly slow flowing rivers and streams, often moving to the coast in winter. **Distribution** Widespread resident except north to central Scotland.

Green Woodpecker *Picus viridis* (family Picidae) 32cm (12½in) Largest and immediately identifiable woodpecker. **Flight** Alternately rising with a few wing-beats and dipping with wings closed. **Voice** A loud, rapid 'laughing' call. **Habitat** Mainly deciduous woodland but roams to open country feeding mostly on the ground. **Distribution** Resident north to central Scotland, but absent from Ireland.

Great Spotted Woodpecker *Dendrocopos major* 23cm (9in) Strikingly patterned black and white with red undertail coverts. **Flight** Similar to Green. **Voice** A loud 'tchick'; also in spring a 'drumming' noise produced by rapidly striking a dead branch. **Habitat** Woodland. **Distribution** Resident in most areas, but only a casual visitor to Ireland.

Lesser Spotted Woodpecker *Dendrocopos minor* 14·5cm (5¾in) Small size and barred back and wings distinctive. **Flight** Similar to Green. **Voice** A shrill 'pee-pee-pee'; also 'drums'. **Habitat** Woodland. **Distribution** Widespread resident, absent from Scotland and Ireland.

Wryneck *Jynx torquilla* 16·5cm (6½in) Looks more like a grey-brown passerine than a woodpecker. **Flight** Slow and undulating. **Voice** A shrill 'quee-quee-quee'. **Habitat** Woods, open parkland, orchards and gardens. **Distribution** Rare summer visitor, almost extinct in south-east England, but a few pairs recently in Scotland. Regular in small numbers on autumn passage, mostly on the east coast.

Nightjar ♂

Swift

Kingfisher

Green Woodpecker ♂

Great Spotted Woodpecker ♂

Lesser Spotted Woodpecker ♂

Wryneck

Larks, Swallow and martins

Woodlark *Lullula arborea* (family Alaudidae) 15cm (6in) Shorter tailed than larger Skylark and has conspicuous white eye-stripes. **Flight** Normal flight undulating, also has a circular song flight at a constant height. **Voice** Melodious, though less powerful than Skylark; call note 'titloo-eet'. **Habitat** Varied, but with scattered trees and scrub. **Distribution** Resident, breeding locally in southern England and Wales.

Skylark *Alauda arvensis* 17·5cm (7in) Generally streaky brown, slightly crested with white outer tail. **Flight** Strong and slightly undulating, performs the well-known song-flight. **Voice** A sustained song often from great height. Flight note 'chirrup'. **Habitat** Open country. **Distribution** Common resident throughout Great Britain and Ireland.

Shorelark *Eremophila alpestris* 16·5cm (6½in) Bold patterning on head, duller in winter and not so pronounced in females and immatures, distinguishes it from other larks. **Flight** Similar to Skylark. **Voice** A shrill 'tsissup'. **Habitat** Beaches, saltings and stubble fields near the coast. **Distribution** Winter visitor, mainly to the east coast south of Yorkshire; occasional elsewhere.

Swallow *Hirundo rustica* (family Hirundinidae) 19cm (7½in) Easily recognized and distinguished from other hirundines by its long tail streamers, chestnut throat and forehead, though these features are less pronounced in young birds. **Flight** Graceful and aerobatic; normally only settles on the ground when collecting nest material. **Voice** A rapid twitter. **Habitat** Open country where buildings are available for nest sites and usually close to water. **Distribution** Summer visitor throughout Great Britain and Ireland.

House Martin *Delichon urbica* 12·5cm (5in) Entire underparts white, contrasting with the mainly blue-black upperparts with a white rump. In some places large numbers nest close together. **Flight** Often flies higher than Swallow. **Voice** A clear 'chirrp'. **Habitat** Open country; mostly nesting on buildings but also uses cliff faces. **Distribution** Summer visitor throughout much of Great Britain and Ireland.

Sand Martin *Riparia riparia* 12cm (4¾in) Smaller than Swallow with brown upperparts and a distinct brown chest band. **Flight** Rather more fluttering and erratic than Swallow. **Voice** A harsh 'tchrrip'. **Habitat** Open country where river banks, cuttings and sand and gravel pits provide suitable nesting places, sometimes for large colonies. **Distribution** Summer visitor to much of Great Britain and Ireland; scarce in the extreme north-west.

Woodlark

Skylark

Shorelark

Swallow

House Martin

Sand Martin

Crows family Corvidae

Raven *Corvus corax* 64 cm (25 in) Our largest crow, having a massive bill and shaggy throat feathers. **Flight** Powerful; often aerobatic, when overhead the wedge-shaped tail may be seen. **Voice** A deep 'kronking'. **Habitat** Mainly coastal and upland regions. **Distribution** Resident in western and northern areas.

Carrion Crow *Corvus corone* 45 cm (18½ in) All-black plumage. The Hooded Crow, with grey mantle and underparts, replaces the Carrion Crow in Ireland and the Scottish Isles, and outnumbers the Carrion Crow in north Scotland and the Isle of Man. In parts of the Highlands the two forms interbreed. **Flight** Regular wing-beats. **Voice** A croaking 'kraah'. **Habitat** Almost ubiquitous. **Distribution** Resident throughout Great Britain and Ireland.

Rook *Corvus frugilegus* 46 cm (18 in) Adult easily separated from Carrion Crow by the pale greyish patch of bare skin around the base of the bill and the baggy thigh feathers. **Flight** Direct with steady wing-beats; wheels around rookery. **Voice** A harsh 'caw' but has variety of other calls. **Habitat** Agricultural areas with tall trees for colonial nesting. **Distribution** Resident in most areas.

Jackdaw *Corvus monedula* 33 cm (13 in) Its small size, grey nape and ear coverts distinguish this species from the larger crows. **Flight** Faster wing-beats than Rook and Carrion Crow. **Voice** A high pitched 'chak'. **Habitat** Open country having ruins, cliffs and old timber in which the birds nest. **Distribution** Resident throughout Great Britain and Ireland.

Magpie *Pica pica* 46 cm (18 in) Unmistakable with pied plumage and long (up to 25 cm, 10 in) tail. **Flight** Rather slow though with quite rapid wing-beats. **Voice** A harsh 'chak-chak-chak'. **Habitat** Chiefly farmland but increasingly suburban; usually nests in tall hedges. **Distribution** Resident north to central Scotland; locally in the eastern Highlands.

Jay *Garrulus glandarius* 34 cm (13½ in) Brightly patterned though surprisingly well camouflaged in woodland. **Flight** Rather jerky with rounded wings; a conspicuous white rump. **Voice** A harsh 'skraaak'. **Habitat** Mainly woodland. **Distribution** Resident north to central Scotland but absent from some lowland counties. In Ireland it is absent from the far west and local in parts of its range.

Chough *Pyrrhocorax pyrrhocorax* 39·5 cm (15½ in) More slender than Jackdaw and having a curved red bill and legs. **Voice** A high-pitched 'kyow'. **Habitat** Rocky coasts, but inland in some mountainous areas. **Distribution** Resident, restricted to parts of Ireland, Wales, the Isle of Man and the south Inner Hebrides.

Raven

Carrion Crow

Rook

Jackdaw

Magpie

Jay

Chough

Tits family Paridae

Great Tit *Parus major* 14cm (5½in) Our largest tit and a familiar garden bird, with a broad black band down the centre of its bright yellow underparts. **Flight** Usually of short duration from tree to tree; undulating may rise high over longer distances. **Voice** Main song a loud repeated 'teacher, teacher'; a wide variety of other notes. **Habitat** Woodlands, gardens and hedgerows. **Distribution** Resident in all areas.

Blue Tit *Parus caeruleus* 11·5cm (4½in) Bright blue cap marks it out from other tits. Yellow underparts. **Flight** Similar to Great, but weaker, more fluttering. **Voice** Main note a scolding 'tsee-tsee-tsee'. **Habitat** Similar to Great, though regularly wanders to reedbeds and wasteland in winter. **Distribution** Resident throughout Great Britain and Ireland except Orkney and Shetland.

Coal Tit *Parus ater* 11·5cm (4½in) The white nape-patch and double white wing-bars distinguish it from other tits of the same size. Often moves in Treecreeper fashion on the trunks of trees. **Flight** As for Blue. **Voice** A piping 'tsu-i' and a rather Goldcrest-like 'tsee-tsee-tsee'. Song has repeated double note pattern of Great, but is thinner and faster. **Habitat** Mainly woodland, especially conifers. **Distribution** Resident in all areas except Orkney and Shetland.

Crested Tit *Parus cristatus* 11·5cm (4½in) Speckled black and white crest separates it from all other species of this size. **Flight** As for Blue. **Voice** A low purring 'choor-r-r'. **Habitat** Coniferous woodland especially mature Scots pine. **Distribution** Resident, restricted to the eastern Highlands of Scotland.

Marsh Tit *Parus palustris* 11·5cm (4½in) Combination of black cap and plain brown upperparts distinguishes Marsh from all others, except Willow. See Willow for differences. **Flight** As for Blue. **Voice** Various calls; a loud 'pitcheew' positively identifies this species. **Habitat** Typically deciduous woods, especially oak, also hedgerows. **Distribution** Resident in England and Wales, but absent from Scotland (except Berwick) and Ireland.

Willow Tit *Parus montanus* 11·5cm (4½in) Differs from Marsh in having a matt rather than glossy crown, and a pale patch in the closed secondaries. These distinctions are often difficult to see, and young or worn Marsh and Willows may look very similar. The safest clues are the distinctive 'pitcheew' note of Marsh and the repeated nasal note of Willow. **Flight** As for Great. **Voice** Various calls of which a harsh nasal 'dzee-dzee-dzee-dzee' is typical. **Habitat** Wood, copses, hedgerows, but a preference for damp areas where nest holes are excavated in rotten trunks and branches. **Distribution** Similar to Marsh though extends into south-west Scotland.

Great Tit

Blue Tit

Coal Tit

Crested Tit

Marsh Tit

Willow Tit

Long-tailed Tit *Aegithalos caudatus* (family Aegithalidae) 14cm (5½in) A small, black, white and pinkish bird with a tail over half its total length. Often remains in family parties in autumn and winter, sometimes mixing with other tits, Goldcrests and Treecreepers. **Flight** Rather laboured and undulating. **Voice** Typical notes include a repeated, short, hard 'tut' and a thin 'zee-zee-zee'. **Habitat** Hedgerows, bushy heaths, scrub and woodland. **Distribution** Resident throughout Great Britain and Ireland, except for the extreme north of Scotland.

Nuthatch *Sitta europaea* (family Sittidae) 14cm (5½in) Blue-grey upperparts and mainly buffish chestnut underparts. Has a long straight bill and surprising agility when ascending or descending tree-trunks. **Flight** Usually short between trees. **Voice** Includes a loud ringing 'chwit-chwit' and a repeated clear piping note. **Habitat** Woodland or parkland and gardens with large trees. **Distribution** Resident in most of England and Wales, but absent from Scotland and Ireland.

Treecreeper *Certhia familiaris* (family Certhiidae) 12·5cm (5in) Upperparts streaked brown in contrast with the white underparts. Long curved bill used for extracting insects and spiders from bark crevices as it climbs trunks. Often moves through woods climbing up and around one tree, then flying down to the base of the next. **Flight** Rather tit-like. **Voice** A thin high-pitched 'tsee'. **Habitat** As for Nuthatch. **Distribution** Resident in most areas.

Wren *Troglodytes troglodytes* (family Troglodytidae) 9·5cm (3¾in) One of our most familiar birds with russet brown plumage and a short, usually erect tail. **Flight** Straight, with whirring wings. **Voice** A hard scolding 'tic-tic-tic', and a loud, shrill hurried song. **Habitat** Low cover in a great variety of country. **Distribution** Resident throughout Great Britain and Ireland.

Dipper *Cinclus cinclus* (family Cinclidae) 18cm (7in) Has the shape of a giant Wren, with a conspicuous white throat and chestnut belly. Wades, and can feed under water, either swimming or walking on the bottom. **Flight** Rapid and usually low. **Voice** A metallic 'clink'. **Habitat** Fast-flowing streams and rivers. **Distribution** Resident in western and northern areas.

Bearded Reedling *Panurus biarmicus* (family Timaliidae) 16·5cm (6½in) Mainly tawny brown, long-tailed, males having conspicuous head markings. **Flight** Rather laboured and undulating on whirring wings. **Voice** A metallic 'tching-tching'. **Habitat** Large reedbeds for breeding, though in winter it may occur in much smaller areas. **Distribution** Resident which has recently spread from East Anglia to nest in several southern counties, and suitable sites elsewhere.

Long-tailed Tit

Nuthatch

Treecreeper

Wren

Dipper

Bearded Reedling

♂

♀

Thrushes, chats family Turdidae

Mistle Thrush *Turdus viscivorus* 27cm (10½in) Larger and greyer than Song with bolder breast spots, white underwing and tips to outer tail. **Flight** Strong and level despite frequent closures of the wings. **Voice** A harsh 'churring', and a loud song of short phrases, rather like Blackbird in tone. **Habitat** Woods, farmland, parks and gardens. **Distribution** Resident, breeding in all areas.

Fieldfare *Turdus pilaris* 25·5cm (10in) Its grey head, neck and rump, and chestnut back are distinctive. **Flight** Similar to slightly larger Mistle Thrush. **Voice** A harsh repeated 'chack-chack'. **Habitat** Open country with hedges and copses of berry-bearing shrubs. **Distribution** Winter visitor but in recent years has nested several times in Scotland and the northern Isles and exceptionally in northern England.

Song Thrush *Turdus philomelos* 23cm (9in) Smaller and browner than Mistle, and more buffish on the flanks. **Flight** Fast and direct. **Voice** Song is a series of repeated musical phrases, call note a thin 'sipp'. **Habitat** Varied, where there is enough cover for nesting, often close to human habitation. **Distribution** Resident throughout Great Britain and Ireland.

Redwing *Turdus iliacus* 21cm (8¼in) Darker brown than Song Thrush with a pale eye-stripe and reddish flanks. **Flight** As for Song but reddish flanks and axillaries may be distinguished. **Voice** A thin 'seeip', often heard from migrants overhead at night. **Habitat** Breeds in woodland; frequents open and wooded country in winter. **Distribution** Chiefly a widespread winter visitor, but in recent years has increasingly nested in Scotland.

Ring Ouzel *Turdus torquatus* 24cm (9½in) Rather like Blackbird but both sexes have a white gorget on the breast (less obvious in female) and a pale wing-patch. **Flight** Rapid and direct. **Voice** A loud 'tac-tac-tac', and a loud, clear, but limited song. **Habitat** Breeds mainly on mountain and moorland, particularly where there are patches of scrub; often seen near the coast when on passage. **Distribution** Summer visitor in western and northern areas.

Blackbird *Turdus merula* 25cm (10in) One of our most striking and well-known birds, the female being browner. **Flight** Rather direct, though wavering over short distances. **Voice** A rich fluty song, an anxious 'tchook', and the familiar screaming chatter alarm cry. **Habitat** Varied, providing there is enough cover for nesting. **Distribution** Resident throughout Great Britain and Ireland.

Mistle Thrush

Fieldfare

Redwing

Song Thrush

Blackbird ♂

Blackbird ♀

Ring Ouzel ♂

♀

Wheatear *Oenanthe oenanthe* 14·5cm (5¼in) An alert and active bird. **Flight** Low and direct. Regardless of sex or age the white rump and tail sides are immediately visible. **Voice** A grating 'chack-chack' and a short, warbling song. **Habitat** Moorland, heaths, downs and coastal turf. **Distribution** Widespread summer visitor in all areas except central and south-east England.

Stonechat *Saxicola torquata* 12·5cm (5in) A striking species easily located as it generally perches in conspicuous positions. Quick movements, flicks tail and wings. **Flight** Low with fast wing-beats, showing dark tail and white wing-patches. **Voice** A repeated harsh 'tsak-tsak' resembling small pebbles being knocked together. **Habitat** Special liking for gorse; commons, coastal headlands, rough hillsides and heaths. **Distribution** Resident mainly in western and northern coastal counties.

Whinchat *Saxicola rubetra* 12·5cm (5in) Similar in habits to Stonechat. Pale eye-stripe is a useful distinguishing mark. **Flight** Jerky, with white showing on the sides of the tail close to its base. **Voice** A grating 'tic-tic', a liquid 'tu', and a short warbling song. **Habitat** Rough grassland, heaths and moors, young conifer plantations. **Distribution** Summer visitor to much of Great Britain, but only local in Ireland and south-east England.

Redstart *Phoenicurus phoenicurus* 14cm (5½in) An active species which constantly quivers its reddish tail in an up-and-down motion. **Flight** Reddish tail striking. **Voice** A Willow Warbler-like 'hooeet', and a liquid 'tooick'. Brief musical song with jangling finish. **Habitat** Breeds in deciduous woodland. **Distribution** Summer visitor to most of Great Britain though rare in Ireland.

Black Redstart *Phoenicurus ochruros* 14cm (5½in) The black or greyish underparts distinguish it from Redstart. **Flight** Reddish tail conspicuous. **Voice** Scolding 'tucc-tucc', and a quick warbly song. **Habitat** Buildings, especially power stations and factory areas, cliffs and quarries. **Distribution** A scarce summer visitor, breeding mainly in south-east England; some overwinter. Regular passage migrant on east and south coasts.

Nightingale *Luscinia megarhynchos* 16·5cm (6½in) A skulking bird with all-brown upperparts and a rufous tail. **Flight** Usually low with tail conspicuous. **Voice** Loud, rich and varied song, pausing between phrases. Sings by day and night; alarm notes harsh and grating. **Habitat** Mainly woodland with thick undergrowth. **Distribution** Summer visitor, mainly south and east of a line from Dorset to the Wash.

Robin *Erithacus rubecula* 14cm (5½in) Adults unmistakable; speckled immatures, however, lack the red breast. **Flight** Usually low. **Voice** A loud warbly song and a 'tic-tic' note. **Habitat** Varied, where cover is available. **Distribution** Resident, breeding in all areas except Shetland.

Wheatear

Stonechat

Whinchat

Redstart

Black Redstart

Nightingale

Robin

Robin juvenile

Warblers family Sylviidae

Grasshopper Warbler *Locustella naevia* 12·5cm (5in) Difficult to see, slips through cover. Has strongly streaked brown upperparts and a rounded tail. **Flight** Usually of short duration, the bird quickly seeking cover. **Voice** A characteristic reeling song, often heard after dark as well as by day. **Habitat** Varies from marshland to heaths and young conifer plantations, but always with thick undergrowth. **Distribution** Summer visitor to all counties except parts of north Scotland and the Isles.

Reed Warbler *Acrocephalus scirpaceus* 12·5cm (5in) Uniform brown upperparts and light buff underparts. No distinct eye-stripe. **Flight** Usually of short duration with a spread tail. **Voice** A low 'churr' and a deliberate song of repeated, mostly harsh, sounds. **Habitat** Reedbeds. **Distribution** Summer visitor to England and Wales, though absent or local in the west and north.

Sedge Warbler *Acrocephalus schoenobaenus* 12·5cm (5in) Has boldly streaked upperparts and a conspicuous whitish eye-stripe. **Flight** Tail is spread during short flights, while the tawny rump is apparent. **Voice** A loud 'tuc-tuc', and mixed 'churrings'. Song lacks the steady rhythm of Reed Warbler, is faster, more varied, sometimes imitating other birds. **Habitat** Mainly thick vegetation near water. **Distribution** Summer visitor to most of Great Britain and Ireland.

Blackcap *Sylvia atricapilla* 14cm (5½in) Male's black, and female's red-brown, caps are distinctive. Both have grey-brown upperparts and pale underparts. **Flight** Usually reluctant to fly any distance and quickly retires into cover. **Voice** A distinctive scolding 'tchack', while the song is easy, rich, and tuneful. Also has a faster sub-song, much like the song of Garden Warbler. **Habitat** Generally wooded areas, large gardens and overgrown hedges. **Distribution** Summer visitor, breeding in Great Britain except the far north, less commonly in Ireland, except the north-west. Has in recent years shown an increasing tendency to overwinter and may come to bird tables.

Garden Warbler *Sylvia borin* 14cm (5½in) Plumage uniform and lacking any distinctive features. Rather plump with a round head and short bill. **Flight** Similar to Blackcap. **Voice** Song is faster and more uniform than Blackcap's song, but similar to Blackcap's sub-song. Calls low and harsh. **Habitat** Woods, bushy commons, heaths, large gardens and parks. **Distribution** Summer visitor, breeding throughout Great Britain, apart from the extreme north-west. In Ireland, extremely local, mainly in the Shannon valley.

Grasshopper Warbler

Reed Warbler

Sedge Warbler

Blackcap

♀

♂

Garden Warbler

Whitethroat *Sylvia communis* 14cm (5½in) Male has a grey cap and cheeks contrasting with a white throat and a rufous patch in the wings. Female has the white throat under a brown head. Tail rather long, white-edged. **Flight** Rather jerky and short, often diving into cover. **Voice** Various scolding notes. Rapid chattering song often delivered during a dancing song flight. **Habitat** Open areas with thick cover of hedgerows, brambles, nettles, scrub or osiers. **Distribution** Summer visitor breeding throughout Great Britain and Ireland.

Lesser Whitethroat *Sylvia curruca* 13·5cm (5¼in) Sexes similar, more compact than Whitethroat, having greyer upperparts and a dark patch on the ear coverts. **Flight** As for Whitethroat. **Voice** A rather Blackcap-like 'tchak'. The song is a distinctive fast rattle on one note, usually preceded by a short warble. **Habitat** Similar to Whitethroat but often amongst taller growth. **Distribution** Summer visitor, breeding mainly in south-eastern England, locally elsewhere; absent from Scotland and Ireland.

Dartford Warbler *Sylvia undata* 12·5cm (5in) A skulking dark plum-aged bird with a long, often cocked or fanned tail. **Flight** Weak, undulating action with fast wing-beats and a bobbing tail. **Voice** A scolding 'tchir-r' song rather Whitethroat-like. **Habitat** Heath areas with gorse. **Distribution** Resident, breeding in a few southern counties principally Dorset and Hampshire.

Willow Warbler *Phylloscopus trochilus* 11cm (4¼in) Plumage some-what more greenish above and yellowish beneath than Chiffchaff, but distinction not clear cut. Legs pale; Chiffchaff's legs are usually dark. **Flight** Rather jerky. **Voice** A gentle 'hoo-eet', and a sweet descending song ending with a flourish. **Habitat** Varied; woods, and more open areas with trees, tall scrub, hedges. **Distribution** Summer visitor, breeding in all counties, except Shetland.

Chiffchaff *Phylloscopus collybita* 11cm (4¼in) Best distinguished from Willow by its song. **Flight** As for Willow. **Voice** Song the familiar steadily repeated 'chiff-chaff'; call 'hweet'. **Habitat** More restricted to mature woodland than Willow Warbler. **Distribution** Summer visitor, breeding in most counties, but local in north-east, with a few overwintering.

Wood Warbler *Phylloscopus sibilatrix* 12·5cm (5in) Brighter green back than two previous warblers, yellow throat and breast, white belly and marked eye-stripe. **Flight** As for Willow. **Voice** An accelerating trill and a repeated plaintive 'piu'; usual call a similar note uttered singly. **Habitat** Mature woodlands. **Distribution** Summer visitor to most of Britain; rather local in the south-east and extreme north-west, and very local in Ireland.

Whitethroat

Lesser Whitethroat

Dartford Warbler

Willow Warbler

Chiffchaff

Wood Warbler

Goldcrest *Regulus regulus* (family Regulidae) 9cm (3½in) Very small and compact, plump and fine-billed. Double white wing-bar, and on adults bright crown. Often mixes with tit flocks outside the breeding season. **Flight** Rather tit-like. **Voice** Call a high, thin 'zee-zee-zee-zee'. Song is high-pitched and short, a repeated double note, followed by a flourish. **Habitat** Typically coniferous woods, local in deciduous areas; many move to hedgerows and scrub in winter. **Distribution** Resident in all counties except Orkney and Shetland.

Firecrest *Regulus ignicapillus* 9cm (3½in) Similar build and habits to Goldcrest from which it is best distinguished by the striking head pattern of black and white eye-stripes. Also greener above, whiter below, with a bronzy shade on the sides of the neck. **Flight** As for Goldcrest. **Voice** Call a less high-pitched 'zit'. **Habitat** Breeds in mixed woods, especially with spruce and larch; otherwise in a variety of habitats with trees and bushes. **Distribution** Mainly a passage migrant in England; scarce elsewhere; since 1961 has bred in southern counties; is increasing and spreading.

Flycatchers family Muscicapidae

Spotted Flycatcher *Muscicapa striata* 14cm (5½in) The upright stance, and rapid flights from the same perch after insects immediately identify this bird as a flycatcher. The sexes are similar, mouse-brown with slight streaking on crown and breast. **Flight** Flutters and twists after insects; longer flights are rapid and undulating. **Voice** Main call a Robin-like 'tzee'; song simply a few squeaky notes. **Habitat** Open woodland, gardens, parkland. **Distribution** Summer visitor.

Pied Flycatcher *Ficedula hypoleuca* 13cm (5in) The male in summer plumage is a distinctive black and white; females and males in autumn are brown and white. The white wing-patch and outer tail prevent confusion with slightly larger Spotted. **Flight** Unlike that species it rarely returns to the same perch when feeding. Tail is constantly flirted. **Voice** A loud 'whit' and a 'wheet'; song short and pleasing with Redstart-like trill. **Habitat** Well-developed woodland, often along valleys in hilly country. **Distribution** Summer visitor, breeding in western and northern counties to the central Highlands. Occurs in Ireland only whilst on passage, when it is also regular on the English east coast.

Dunnock *Prunella modularis* (family Prunellidae) 14·5cm (5¾in) A plump bird with a thin bill, streaked back and grey head and underparts. Usually keeps in or close to cover. Frequently flicks its wings. **Flight** Usually low and over a short distance. **Voice** A shrill 'seep'; song a weak pleasant jingle. **Habitat** Hedgerows, bushy areas, scrub, open woods with undergrowth. **Distribution** Resident throughout Great Britain and Ireland.

Goldcrest

Firecrest

Spotted Flycatcher

Pied Flycatcher

Dunnock

Pipits, wagtails family Motacillidae

Meadow Pipit *Anthus pratensis* 14·5cm (5¾in) Streaked, with a rather long, white-edged tail; spends most of its time on the ground. Rather similar to Tree from which it is best distinguished by song. **Flight** Rather jerky, rising and falling; often sings in climbing flight and 'parachute' descent. **Voice** A thin 'tseep' repeated thin notes becoming more musical and ending in a trill. **Habitat** Rough open country. **Distribution** Resident.

Tree Pipit *Anthus trivialis* 15cm (6in) Slightly larger than Meadow, and of a warmer buffish-brown colour, but voice is best distinction. **Flight** Has a song flight whilst descending to a perch, usually in a tree. **Voice** A loud, at times shrill, song. Less hurried, sweeter than Meadow; call a hoarse 'teez'. **Habitat** Heaths, hillsides and commons with scattered trees, woodland glades and edges. **Distribution** Summer visitor, breeding in most areas; not Ireland.

Rock Pipit *Anthus spinoletta* 16·5cm (6½in) Larger and darker than the two previous species, with dark legs and dusky, not white, outer tail feathers. **Flight** As for Meadow and has a similar song flight. **Voice** Call note 'tsup', not as thin and squeaky as Meadow. Song resembles Meadow but louder and fuller. **Habitat** Rocky coasts. **Distribution** Resident on all coasts except low-lying eastern ones, though winters there.

Pied/White Wagtail *Motacilla alba* 18cm (7in) Contrasting black and white plumage, long slender build and continual tail movements quickly identify this species. The White Wagtail has a pale grey back and rump, but in autumn the races are very similar. **Flight** Undulating. **Voice** A loud 'tchizzik' call, and a twittering song. **Habitat** Open country with buildings, banks, etc., to provide nest sites usually near water. **Distribution** Pied a resident, breeding in all counties; White seen chiefly on passage, occasionally nests in far north.

Grey Wagtail *Motacilla cinerea* 18cm (7in) Blue-grey upperparts, yellowish rump and longer tail prevent confusion with Yellow. **Voice** Usual call rather shorter, higher-pitched than other wagtails. **Habitat** Nests usually beside fast-flowing water, spreading to a variety of sites near water in winter. **Distribution** Resident in most counties; local or absent except outside breeding season from eastern England.

Yellow/Blue-headed Wagtail *Motacilla flava* 16·5cm (6½in) Shorter tail than Grey and a greenish brown back. **Flight** Undulating. **Voice** A shrill 'tseweeep'; song a simple warble. **Habitat** Lowland meadows, marshland and some heaths, usually near water. **Distribution** Summer visitor, breeding throughout much of England; local or absent elsewhere except on passage. The Blue-headed Wagtail or variants breed very locally in the south-east; occasionally elsewhere.

Meadow Pipit

Tree Pipit

Rock Pipit

Pied Wagtail ♂

White Wagtail

Grey Wagtail
summer ♂

Yellow Wagtail ♂

Blue-headed Wagtail ♂

Waxwing *Bombycilla garrulus* (family Bombycillidae) 18cm (7in) Prominently crested with bright plumage. **Flight** Similar to Starling, and has a grey rump and lower back. **Voice** A trilling 'sirrr'. **Habitat** Associated with berry-bearing shrubs and trees wherever these occur; commons, parks, gardens. **Distribution** Winter visitor, mainly to eastern counties with occasional 'invasions' westwards.

Red-backed Shrike *Lanius collurio* (family Laniidae) 17cm (6¾in) Striking plumage and habit of sitting on prominent perches aid identification. **Flight** Rather dipping with pointed wings and a long tail; can hover, and darts about to catch flies. **Voice** A harsh 'chack-chack'. **Habitat** Scrubby commons, bramble patches and thickets. **Distribution** Summer visitor, much decreased in numbers and now only breeding in south-east England.

Starling *Sturnus vulgaris* (family Sturnidae) 21·5cm (8½in) One of our best known birds. **Flight** Direct and rapid with frequent glides. **Voice** Common call a harsh descending 'tcheer'. A rather warbly song interspersed with whistles and rattles. Good mimic. **Habitat** From cities to remote coasts. **Distribution** Resident.

Hawfinch *Coccothraustes coccothraustes* (family Fringillidae) 18cm (7in) A large finch with a thick neck and bill and secretive habits. **Flight** Rapid wing-beats and undulating. **Voice** An explosive 'tzik'. **Habitat** Mature deciduous woods, gardens and orchards. **Distribution** Resident, breeding locally in England, Wales and southern Scotland; an occasional visitor to Ireland.

Greenfinch *Carduelis chloris* 14·5cm (5¾in) A plump greenish bird with yellow wing-patches. **Flight** Slightly undulating, the yellow wing-patches and tail sides being noticeable. **Voice** Usual call a rapid musical twitter, a wheezing 'tswee' from males in spring; the song, a medley of twittering notes, is often delivered in a slow-flapping 'butterfly' flight. **Habitat** All areas with trees and bushes. **Distribution** Resident.

Goldfinch *Carduelis carduelis* 12cm (4¾in) The sexes are similarly brightly coloured, the young streaky grey but showing the bold wing and tail patterns. **Flight** Rather dancing with a yellow wing-bar. **Voice** Usual call a repeated liquid note; song a pleasant liquid twittering. **Habitat** Similar to Greenfinch, often feeds on low plants, thistle, etc. **Distribution** Resident, breeding in all counties except for the north and north-west of Scotland.

Siskin *Carduelis spinus* 12cm (4¾in) Females are greyer with more streaks beneath and no black on the head. **Flight** Buoyant, with yellow sides to tail, and wing-bar. **Voice** Shrill and twittering calls. **Habitat** Breeds in coniferous woods, spreads in winter to alders and birches, and increasingly, gardens. **Distribution** Resident, nesting mainly in Scotland; locally further south. Widespread in winter.

Waxwing ♀

Red-backed Shrike ♂

♀

Starling

Hawfinch ♂

Greenfinch ♂

Goldfinch

Siskin ♂

Linnet *Acanthis cannabina* 13cm (5¼in) Male has chestnut back and grey head with, in summer, red crown and breast; female and young duller. All show white feather edgings in wing and tail. **Flight** Rapid, often wavering and dancing. **Voice** A rapid twittering call and pleasant song. **Habitat** Breeds in scrub thickets and hedgerows, spreads to a variety of open country in autumn and winter. **Distribution** Resident, breeding throughout Great Britain and Ireland.

Twite *Acanthis flavirostris* 13·5cm (5¼in) More tawny with heavier dark streaking than female and young Linnet, and an orange-buff face. In winter the bill is yellow. **Flight** Similar to Linnet. **Voice** Calls a nasal 'tsweet' and a Linnet-like twitter. **Habitat** Breeds in moorland and hill areas. Also shore, saltings and coastal fields in winter. **Distribution** Resident, breeding mainly in the west of Scotland and Ireland; locally elsewhere in Scotland and the Pennines. Regular in winter on the English coast between Lincoln and Sussex.

Redpoll *Acanthis flammea* 13cm (5in) Small, plump, feeding acrobatically in trees. Males differ from females in summer in having a pinkish breast and rump. **Flight** Light and often high. **Voice** Call a metallic twittering 'chuch-uch-uch'; trilling song sometimes given in a circular song flight. **Habitat** Mainly birch woods and conifers. **Distribution** Resident, breeding in most parts except central southern England, more widespread in winter.

Bullfinch *Pyrrhula pyrrhula* 14·5cm (5¾in) Both sexes are unmistakable. Young duller with brown cap. **Flight** Undulating; white rump clearly visible. **Voice** Call a soft piping 'peu'. **Habitat** Areas with plenty of thick cover. **Distribution** Resident in most areas.

Crossbill *Loxia curvirostra* 16·5cm (6½in) Crossed mandibles may be seen at close range. **Flight** Rapid and undulating; heavy head and forked tail visible. **Voice** A loud 'chip-chip', both in flight and when feeding. **Habitat** Coniferous woodland. **Distribution** Resident in the Highlands, parts of East Anglia, Hampshire and locally elsewhere. Following periodic eruptions may breed in many other areas.

Chaffinch *Fringilla coelebs* 15cm (6in) Our commonest finch. **Flight** Wing-bars and white outer tail feathers noticeable. **Voice** A loud 'pink'; in spring a clear 'whee', and a short, loud song accelerating to a final flourish. **Habitat** Varied, provided that bushes or trees are available for nesting. **Distribution** Resident, breeding throughout Great Britain and Ireland.

Brambling *Fringilla montifringilla* 14·5cm (5¾in) Sexes rather similar in winter. **Flight** Conspicuous white rump. **Voice** A metallic 'tsweek', or 'chuc-chuc-chuc'. **Habitat** Woods, especially beech, rough weedy areas, stubble, etc. **Distribution** Winter visitor to most parts.

Linnet

Twite

Redpoll

Bullfinch

Crossbill

Chaffinch

Brambling
winter

Buntings family Emberizidae

Corn Bunting *Emberiza calandra* 18cm (7in) A plump, uniformly brown-streaked bird with a large bill. **Flight** Heavy often with legs dangling. **Voice** An abrupt, dry 'quit'; song ends with a sound like a small bunch of keys jangling. **Habitat** Open farmland, commons, waste land. **Distribution** Resident, breeding mainly in east coast counties; rather local in the west and in Ireland.

Yellowhammer *Emberiza citrinella* 16·5cm (6½in) Female and juvenile less yellow than the bright male. **Flight** Chestnut rump and white outer tail feathers conspicuous. **Voice** A metallic 'twink' call; song, commonly written 'a little bit of bread and no cheese', consists of a high-pitched series ending in a longer note. **Habitat** Farmland, hedgerow, heath, scrub, young plantations. **Distribution** Resident, breeding in all areas.

Cirl Bunting *Emberiza cirlus* 16·5cm (6½in) Male easily separated from Yellowhammer by bold patterning, females by their olive-brown, not chestnut, rump. **Flight** Rather dipping. **Voice** A thin 'zit'; song a brief metallic rattle on one note. **Habitat** Pasture and other open areas with trees, hedges, and scrub. **Distribution** Resident, breeding locally in south and south-west England.

Reed Bunting *Emberiza schoeniclus* 15cm (6in) Females and young are duller than male in breeding plumage, but have easily seen eye and moustachial stripes. **Flight** Rather jerky with white outer tail feathers. **Voice** A loud 'chink', and a short squeaky song. **Habitat** Mainly damp areas with plentiful cover, increasingly in drier areas such as farmland, rough waste, heath. **Distribution** Resident in all areas.

Snow Bunting *Plectrophenax nivalis* 16·5cm (6½in) Females much the same as a winter male, though less white on wings and tail. **Flight** Swift and undulating; white underparts and wing patches conspicuous. **Voice** Calls a rippling 'tiriririp' and a clear, ringing 'teu'. **Habitat** Breeds on barren mountain tops; winters on lower ground, often close to the coast. **Distribution** A few pairs breed in northern Scotland; otherwise a widespread winter visitor.

House Sparrow *Passer domesticus* 14·5cm (5¾in) Highly gregarious. **Flight** Rapid. **Voice** A loud 'chee-ip' and various chirps and twitters. **Habitat** Very varied but usually close to human habitation. **Distribution** Resident, breeding in all areas.

Tree Sparrow *Passer montanus* 14cm (5½in) Unlike more robust House, the sexes are similar. Note brown crown, black cheek spot. **Flight** More agile than House. **Voice** Various short calls including a high-pitched 'teck'. **Habitat** Typically woods and other areas with mature trees. Spreads to open land in winter. **Distribution** Resident, breeding in many areas though only locally in the west.

Corn Bunting

Yellowhammer ♂

Cirl Bunting ♂

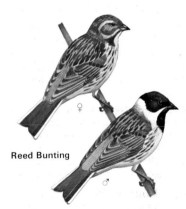

Reed Bunting ♀ ♂

Snow Bunting
winter ♂

Tree Sparrow

House Sparrow ♀ ♂

Glossary

Adult an individual capable of breeding; usually has distinguishing plumage from younger birds

Axillaries the feathers of the wingpit

Carpal joint the 'wrist' of the bird comprising the forward pointing area on the closed wing

Colour phase genetically determined difference in plumage colour within one species. Two or occasionally more distinct colour phases occur in a few species, sometimes with intermediates

Contour feathers feathers which cover the body and which provide the streamlined form and retain body heat

Crepuscular active only at dusk and dawn

Crown upperparts of the head

Ear coverts area immediately behind the eye

Escape the term given to a bird, perhaps genuinely wild, known to have escaped or been genuinely liberated from captivity

First year the period from a bird leaving the nest until the following breeding season

Hood where a distinctive colour covers a major part of the head

Immature usually denoting a bird from a period after leaving the nest (see also juvenile) until it is able to breed. This may be less than a year, but in longer-lived species will be several and in some cases of up to seven years duration. Immatures are often, but not always, recognizable by a distinctive plumage

Invasion when birds normally not or only infrequently seen here arrive suddenly in large numbers

Juvenile the period immediately after leaving the nest (see also immature). Division between juvenile and immature is arbitrary

Mantle the back feathers and immediately adjoining areas, often all of the same general colour

Migration the movement of a bird population from one area to another, frequenting one for breeding and the other for wintering. There are many degrees of migration from the trans-equatorial to merely local movements within our own country

Nape upper part of back of neck

Nostril opening at each side of the base of the upper mandible

Passage migrant a bird not normally breeding or wintering here but regularly seen on migration

Passeriformes the largest order of birds, often referred to as the perching birds

Pectoral muscles the large muscles of the breast; attached to the sternum or breast bone they provide the strong wing movements necessary for flight

Pelagic the deep sea or oceanic habitat, the avifauna of which rarely comes in sight of land except when breeding

Preen gland the oil gland which most birds have and which is situated on the rump

Primaries the largest and main flight feathers, attached to the 'hand'

Raptor another term for bird of prey but excluding owls

Resident one found within a given area throughout the year, though some members of the population will disperse and even make local movements

Rump the area of the lower back and base of the tail

Secondaries the flight feathers of the wing carried on the 'forearm'

Speculum a distinctive area of colour in the wing, most often in ducks

Territory any defended area, mostly for breeding purposes though a few species, best known being the Robin, maintain a winter territory

Index

Figures in **bold** type refer
to the species description
with accompanying
colour illustration.
Figures in *italic* type refer
to other illustrations.